Star Matrix
Silvia Hartmann

1st Paperback Edition June 2021

Published By

DragonRising

www.DragonRising.com

Star Matrix
Discover the true TREASURES & RICHES of YOUR LIFE!

© Silvia Hartmann 2020

First Paperback Edition 2021

ISBN (Paperback): 978-1873-483-046

Published by:

DragonRising Publishing
United Kingdom

DragonRising.com

Other titles by this author:

Modern Energy Tapping

EMO Energy In Motion

Infinite Creativity

Claim Your Inclusive Star Matrix Bonuses

As a thank you for purchasing this Star Matrix book, you have the option to access some fantastic time limited bonuses including Star Matrix videos, online video courses, GoE subscription and downloading your Star Matrix Foundation certificate.

For information see page: 199

Table of Contents

Preface: Star Matrix & Modern Energy

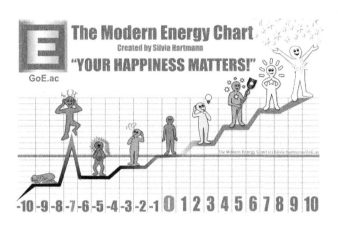

Star Matrix is built on the principles of Modern Energy created by Silvia Hartmann.

If you are unfamiliar with Modern Energy, please download and read Silvia Hartmann's **Modern Energy (r)Evolution**, which is the free concise introduction to the most foundational concepts of Modern Energy: GoE.ac/Revolution

Should you come across a phrase, concept or term that is unfamiliar to you, you can also look it up in the Guild of Energist's A-Z of Modern Energy here: GoE.ac/A-Z/

By purchasing this book you have automatically gained free GoE subscriber benefits including the highly recommended Modern Energy Foundation course GoE.ac/MEF, and you can also complete the online Star Matrix test to download your personalised GoE Star Matrix Foundation certificate: See page *199*

Welcome to Star Matrix –

the most empowering personal development program in the world.

Introduction To Star Matrix 1ˢᵗ Edition by Silvia Hartmann

I am absolutely delighted to welcome you to Star Matrix - the best personal development method in the world today.

It is the best personal development method in the world today because it is not about my knowledge, but it is about yours.

Star Matrix is about recovering the true Treasures & Riches of YOUR life – consciously becoming aware of what you can do, who you really are, based not on some ancient mythology or modern theory, but on your actual life's experiences.

I have been engaged in hard core personal development for the last forty years, and I have sought that one thing that would make all the difference – permanently, forever, without the need to go into a monastery or stand on one leg pretending to be a crane for the next 25 years.

Something easy, effortless, something glorious that would light me up and never leave me again.

After forty years, I've found it.

In a nutshell, this is it.

- **Your Star Memories are the key to understanding your life.**

They are your real and only Treasures & Riches.

They contain your highest wisdom and your greatest power.

All I have to do is to encourage you to connect with what YOU have already learned in this life.

As simple as it may seem, the very act of bringing your best memories into consciousness and connecting them sets up an automatic process of transformation and empowerment that takes on a life of its own.

- **Star Matrix is the key to unlocking the real truth about who you are, and what you are about in this life.**

9

With hindsight, I realise that this is what I've always been searching for.

Something that would work for me, but further, something that would work for all humans, regardless of what they've been through, regardless of what they were trained to think, regardless of where they came from, or where they are going.

I appreciate that this may sound like a grand claim, yet it has been my experience that empowering people is the right way to go, and there is literally nothing as empowering as to finally get a sense of what you can be, what you can do, and have the proof, because it's already happened, and you were there to experience it.

I can tell a person forever that they are more than they think they are; that they are smarter, more resilient, are far more powerful, even that they have actual super powers, and they won't believe me.

That's fair enough! It's best not to believe too much of what other people say. I'm right on board with that one.

However, when you tell a person to remember a time when an aspect of theirs really was powerful, that's a different kind of evidence.

It is the only kind of evidence that is incontrovertible to each and every individual – their own life experiences.

I can prove that you are MORE.

The proof is in your memories.

You have been on a grand journey of life for a long time.

Now the time has come to start gathering in the harvest.

Your Treasures & Riches await.

Welcome to the journey to the Stars!

With lots of love (and much excitement!)

Silvia

Silvia Hartmann

Creator of Modern Energy & Star Matrix

President, The Guild of Energists GoE

From The Darkness To The Stars

We go through life, and we have a variety of experiences. Contrary to public opinion, we don't just have TRAUMA in our lives. Trauma events are actually rare in comparison, but just like the few radical terrorists in a population of a million perfectly good citizens, trauma has been given all the attention - and this has proven to be extremely unhealthy for everyone, especially in the long run.

The absolute and myopic focus on TRAUMA as the only explanation for why people have problems in life has literally herded us all down the wrong path in the Western World, and has caused a myriad of truly damaging side effects that have increased stress, caused all manner of secondary mental, emotional and physical problems to come into being, and has offered no solution at all for the day to day management of emotional disturbances in perfectly normal people.

The total and EXCLUSIVE focus on only trauma, and more trauma, with a side order of trauma, has also produced a totally skewed picture of what human beings are, how they work, and has structurally prevented useful knowledge to be found that could have been used to help people lead better and happier lives.

So, and in short, trauma events are only one type of events a human being experiences in life.[1]

There are other, equally important events. For example, there are the Guiding Stars - incomplete positive events that "chain" a person to try and repeat the experience. All fetishes, philias, and unhealthy addictions are based not on trauma, but on Guiding Stars, and these problems cannot be solved at all or ever whilst searching for a causative trauma, and not even being aware that such things as Guiding Stars exist in the first place.

There are other classes of events that also play their part in why people do the things they do, and there are the Missing Events, where something should have happened, but it never did.

---

1   If you are interested in Events Psychology, please see "Events Psychology" (DragonRising 2008) on the topic.

The most important events of them all have had literally no attention whatsoever, yet they are absolutely central to the functioning of a normal human being.

- **These are the true Star Events - the highest, most profound, most amazing, most positive experiences in a person's lifetime.**

The Plane Crash Survivors: Only LOVE Remains

I studied the experiences of plane crash survivors just past the turn of the millennium, and was struck by the repeated reports of "the life flashing before your eyes" at the moment of perceived death.

A significant number of survivors reported a very similar experience.

They were terrified and convinced they were about to die, when a great calm overcame them, and then this sequence of memories, bright and clear, would unfold for them – their life flashing before their eyes, as the term would go.

When I questioned people more closely about these sequences of memories, I discovered this:

What flashed was NOT trauma.

Not a single trauma memory "flashed before their eyes."

Not a one.

All that flashed where the HIGH POSITIVE MEMORIES of their lifetime - all that remained, was the memory of LOVE.

Wow.

It blew me away and set me on the path that led to where we are now.

Now we can try and explain this phenomenon away with "the brain being flooded by happy hormones" which caused this extraordinary experience; the fact is that every single one of these survivors cited the experience as completely life changing, entirely beneficial, enlightening, and that they walked away with a different sense of what life is all about that was precious, and a Star Event in its own right.

I work with the reality of our living energy bodies, and have satisfied myself that we do, indeed have an energy system that can survive physical death. I believe that at the moment of perceived death, the most important events are "uploaded" to this energy system that is generally called "the soul" and that only the highest energy events, the Star Memories, make it.

Only love remains.

This is a remarkable thought, and once you consider this, we need to ask urgent questions that relate directly to the meaning of life in general, but our own lives in particular.

> What if by endlessly and EXCLUSIVELY focusing on trauma, we all trampled down the wrong path, and in the wrong direction?

> What if by endlessly and EXCLUSIVELY focusing our attention only on trauma, we missed out on the most important "lessons" of life??

> What if by endlessly and EXCLUSIVELY focusing on trauma, we created literal, physical train tracks in the brain that led to trauma and more trauma - instead of leading in the exact opposite direction, into Star Memories and more Star Memories instead???

And then, there was this:

- **What would happen if we deliberately and, for a time, EXCLUSIVELY, focused on our Star Memories instead?**

Well now.

That's an interesting question.

Indeed, it is a question that immediately took me to considering a person's self esteem, their self concept, self construct, conscious idea of the self.

What if we were to build a self concept not based on trauma events, not based on our shortcomings and failures, but instead, on our Star Events, our highest possible aspects?

Well - if we did that, created a self concept built on our Star Memories, that self concept would be ... the Star Matrix!

The Star Matrix: A Whole New You

The Star Matrix would offer an alternative view on who you are, when all is said and done.

The Star Matrix would give us a totally different way to arrange the memories of our lifetimes, and learn totally different lessons about what life can be, and what we can actually do, feel, and experience as a human being here on Earth.

In even attempting to connect with the Star Memories of our own lifetimes, our real and ONLY "Treasures & Riches," the ONLY memories we remember when our life flashes before our eyes, we have to build new connections in the physical brain.

We would have to travel paths of thought we have never consciously attempted to travel before.

Our thinking about ourselves and our place in this world would have to change.

Our self concepts would have to change. They can't not.

Yes, and that's Star Matrix in a nutshell.

- Take your attention off all the trauma for a change.

- Direct your conscious attention to the high positive experiences of your life.

- Recover your Star Memories.

- Find the connections between them.

- Explore the true wisdom, your personal, experienced, lived **Star Wisdom** that is encapsulated in these high positive memories.

- Access skills, talents and abilities that your aspect have already enacted for real.

- Create brand new shiny connections in your physical brain, and of course, in your living energy body.

- And whilst all of that is going on, notice how the focus on your own high positive memories lifts your mood, empowers your energy body, changes your emotional states for the better.

That, and so, so much more!

The potential benefits for interacting with our Star Memories are mind blowing.

The potential effects this interaction would have on our living energy bodies, and through those, directly on our minds and bodies as well could be … miraculous.

They could be life healing, life changing …

The Star Matrix based self concept would absolutely be a brand new, shining YOU.

Ending The Nightmare Of Trauma – Escaping The Infernal Trauma Trap

At this point, many start to scream, "But you're only brushing all the trauma under the carpet! You need to pull the roots of the trauma, dig in the trauma, only that will heal you!"

This is the exact brain washing, brain washed response from a hundred years of that trauma based psychotherapy nightmare we've all been living in.

People have been digging in trauma for sometimes 30 years or more, 3x a week, and where did that ever get them?

Into enlightenment? Or just more trauma?

That's the "trauma trap" right there.

The reason why your life isn't working is because of trauma.

You need to dig into the trauma in order to release the trauma.

Your life still isn't working?

Aha!

We haven't found the right trauma yet.

We have to dig deeper!

And so it goes on and on and on and on in an endless downward spiral.

In the meantime, all that exclusive focus on trauma depletes the energy system, makes therefore the owner of said energy system ever more emotionally unstable and stressed, and there is no end in sight, ever, because as soon as one trauma is released, the next pops up, and the next and the next and the next ...

It's endless.

There has to be a stop to it, there has to be a different way.

A better way, a new approach.

Star Matrix is it.

Your High Positive Memories – Your Treasures & Riches

The first thing the trauma entrained will say when asked about positive memories is that they have NONE. None at all. Their entire childhood was misery, and because of that, their adolescence was misery as well, followed by misery in young adulthood, and so on, right up to this very moment, here and now, when a thoroughly miserable person sits there, entirely convinced that their entire life was nothing but misery.

This response exists because of the "trauma train tracks in the brain," and most of the time, it really needs a major Star Event, such as "having your life flash before your eyes" as the plane ditches towards the ocean, to "change their minds."

The fact is, however, that if you don't accept that answer, that there was never, ever, anything positive at all in their miserable lives, and you keep asking, "Perhaps you had a moment with nature ... or with an animal ... that was wonderful, beautiful ..." you can see people wrinkling their brows, their eyes start darting here and there, they're really thinking about it, and eventually, a memory will come to them.

"Well, I guess there was that time ... after a party ... the sun came up over the hills and it was so beautiful ..."

Right! Whoohoo! We have a positive memory! It can be done!!!

Now here is a very important feature of positive memories.

- **Positive memories are energy rich, information rich, instantly uplifting - and they are very, very clear.**

Unlike a shattered trauma memory that has been dug and scraped and twisted in a thousand therapy sessions and ten thousand nightmares since it happened, a Star Memory is clear, resonant, strong. Colourful. Lucid. All the six senses are there - what we saw, heard, felt physically, what we scented, tasted, and how that made us feel inside.

- **It is super easy to "remember" a Star Memory.**

It is easy to talk about it in exquisite detail, to walk around in the memory, enter right into it, observe the aspect of that time, to connect with that aspect or to inhabit the aspect.

The entire memory experience is perfectly under conscious control; it is a wonderful experience for the person, wakes them up, raises their energy, and the life skill of how we remember something with brilliant clarity is finally learned in the process of deliberately remembering and talking about Star Memories.

All the skills we need to eventually also be able to deal with trauma memories correctly need to be learned with positive memories first.

When a person knows how to handle positive memories, they are in a much, much better position to deal with any other type of memory as well – of course.

That's a simple, structural fact; so even if we can't persuade people right now that focusing on Star Memories is actually the life healing they've been seeking all along, I am 100% going to make the case for finally preparing people properly and to give them skills and tools they need to be able to walk consciously into some sort of trauma hell. At the moment, people are sent there naked and afraid; with the experience of Star Matrix, they can walk into those memories in a metaphorical space suit and rescue aspects without getting burned in the process.

You want to take charge of your memories, understand how they work, how you work when you access them?

Practice with Star Memories.

Remembering your own Star Memories will give you the memory skills you need to go forward.

Your memory ability will improve radically, regardless of how we want to measure that improvement.

Your own Star Memories will also empower you, free you, give you additional information, strength, and become an enormous treasure chest of resources, inspiration, personal power, hope, and the base for a brand new, sparkling self concept.

It's time for Star Matrix thinking to begin!

The Book of Stars

Essential for and central to Star Matrix is your personal Book Of Stars.

This is a beautiful notebook of your choice in which you will write down your Star Memories as you recover them.

On the very first page, write: "This Book of Stars belongs to (the name you call yourself)."

On the next page, we start with the entries, which are numbered as they occur, starting with No. 1.

I recommend the following format for the entries.

1. **The Number**
2. **The Title**
3. **Short description, keywords, (optional sketches)**
4. **The year when this happened**
5. **The age of the aspect who had the Star Event.**

Example Entry

No. 1 = Sunset Stars Over The Ancient Forest

Leaning against a massive oak tree, looking over the valley forest, seeing the first stars of the night sparkling with the sky banded orange, purple and midnight blue.

1971 – Age 12

- **The Number** helps us make connections between memories later on, and they are also important to help us consciously realise just how many amazingly good experiences we've already had so far, especially once the Book of Stars goes over 100 entries.

- **The Title** allows us to consciously encapsulate the experience in essence.

- **The Description** is a memory aid for later, when there are many, many Star Memories in the Book of Stars.

- **The Sketch** is optional, but many people absolutely love to draw a simple sketch of the MOMENT, what the aspect saw, or a sketch of the aspect inside the moment when the Star Event happened. *Sadly, very many people are totally reversed to drawing, had it beaten out of them in school, but I highly encourage to give it a go. A simple map, a stick figure, it really helps to activate and engage the non-language parts of the brain and the energy system. For step by step instructions, please see the Addendum.*

- **The Year** is there to place the Star Memory into a wider context, as all people alive at that time would share the year, even if their cultural notation is different.

- **The Age** of the aspect is the personal place in time and space on the person's timeline. It can also be used later to find "holes" in the timeline of Star Memories that want to be further investigated, and link together sequences of Star Events for big AHA! moments of a personal nature.

Conscious Awareness & The Starving Millionaire

The Book of Stars is all about conscious awareness and intellectual understanding of our Star Events, and how these have shaped our lives far, far more profoundly than any trauma ever could.

The dates, titles, descriptions, age, numbers are all designed to really help us integrate the Star Memories in consciousness.

Conscious awareness of our Treasures & Riches is of the essence!

I tell the story of the man who had been given a million dollars, which had been placed in his bank account, but nobody told him this so he didn't consciously know it.

As a result, he continued to behave like a homeless man and froze to death one night under a railway bridge in a snow storm even though he was a millionaire.

- **Without conscious awareness of what there really is, we have no chance to build a reality based conscious construct (self concept) of who we really are.**

We cannot use the resources we don't know we have.

We need to "take stock" of what's really been happening so we can understand where we are, as well as what has to happen next.

Proof Positive

When we get into low energy states of stress, anxiety, anger, fear or depression, we lose access to our inner resources.

The Book of Stars is proof positive that you didn't imagine all the amazing experiences, that there really was love in your life, that you really are strong and resilient, and far more magical in every way than you have given yourself credit for.

Low energy aspects can turn to the Book of Stars and find inspiration, wisdom, guidance and strength simply by reviewing some of the entries.

Your Book of Stars also contains profound inspiration for all manner of creativity that is absolutely and 100% your own, based on your own life's experiences.

And when someone comes along and tells us we are worthless and count for nothing, or that we haven't achieved anything in our lives, we can place our hands on our own Book of Stars and simply smile at such a preposterous notion.

The Book of Stars As A Power Object

Filled with beautiful, powerful, high positive memories, the Book of Stars is of course a power object in its own right.

In moments of crisis, we can hold our Book of Stars to our heart, and let the power of our Star Aspects and our Star People stabilise us, inspire us, and lift us.

It's a beautiful thing.

Start YOUR Book of Stars TODAY.

Do not delay.

The sooner you start, the better.

The more Star Memories you recover and inscribe in your Book of Stars, the more powerfully inspirational the whole thing will become, and the more benefits you will gain from this in your personal life, right here, right now.

Especially if you are still involved in all sorts of trauma based therapies, you need your Book of Stars as a counterbalance to all that endless negativity.

The Book of Stars will help your energy system stay strong, and it will give you that missing FOUNDATION upon which you can build a better future.

Important Note: It is never too late to start your Book of Stars. The oldest person to begin so far is 97 years old, and in a nursing home. They are getting amazing pleasure, uplifting and joy each and every day as they add wonderful memories into their Book of Stars.

There is a sense of inherent rightness about creating your Book of Stars. It is not a journal, it is not a diary, it is not a scrap book. It is something else altogether and you will experience this once you start. If there is one book inside of every person, it is their own personal Book of Stars.

This is a notion I would like to leave with you.

Every person has a Book of Stars – even if they haven't written it down yet.

Recovering Positive Memories

At the very heart of Star Matrix is to establish the ability to recover positive memories.

The good news:

- **Recovering positive memories is easy.**

All it takes is to know that good things really did happen to everyone, and not only that, that human beings have the extraordinary capacity to find good experiences even and sometimes especially in the most dire of circumstances.

You, too, have had many, many more Star Memories than you are aware of right now.

We also do not need to start with old childhood memories when we begin.

Let me simply ask you about a MOMENT of pure happiness, bliss, feeling fantastic, feeling on top of the world from any time in the last ten years.

Tell me about a good moment.

Telling Star Memories Out Aloud

Now this is a crucial part of the process of not just recovering positive memories, but of integrating them successfully, and of building new neurological connections in your physical brain.

In the early 1970s, the creator of Project Renaissance, Win Wenger, discovered that when people talk out aloud about their internal experiences, whole new areas of the brain "light up," as opposed to just "thinking about it."

The act of describing what is going on in our minds with linear language engages many more areas of the brain, and really brings memories into consciousness.

So when I say, "Tell me your Star Memory," **I mean this literally.**

Take a moment and tell the story of your Star Memory, your STAR STORY, out aloud into the room.

For example:

> "I was on holiday on this beautiful tropical island. One night, I couldn't sleep, so I went for a walk on the beach. Nobody else was there. Then I had this strange feeling – I turned around and saw a massive shooting star flash across the sky! I felt like I was soaring out of myself and travelling with it, it was a fantastic experience!"

Another example (from a participant of the 1st Star Matrix course):

> "My three year old granddaughter Skye was walking very carefully whilst on a forest walk, clinging to my hand. Then she asked me, "Grandma are you brave of snakes?" I loved that phrasing! I started to laugh and told her, yes, I'm brave of snakes! And we had the most wonderful time in the forest, being brave of all sorts of things!"

Another example of a Star Story:

> "My wife and I were on a road trip, and it got very dark, very quickly so we tried to find a place to stop for the night. It was out in the country, pitch black dark, we just pulled off the road near what we thought was a field. Well, the next morning I opened the door and stepped outside – and we had parked directly in front of this massive field of sun flowers! I've never seen such a sight, sunflowers as far as the eye could see, under this amazing blue sky. It took my breath away."

I hope these examples have "triggered" a resonant Star Memory of your own.

Speak it out aloud!

Then enter it in your Book of Stars.

Fantastic! You have your first Star Memory written down in your Book of Stars.

Now we can do all sorts of wonderful things.

Important Note! Sometimes, the memory of one Star Memory triggers more. Star Memories are stored together, in a part of the warehouse of memories that was rarely visited before.

When many Star Memories come, one after the other, please honour each one by making a quick entry in your Book of Stars, even if you just put down the Number, and the Title. You can fill in the rest later.

The more Star Memories are in your Book of Stars, the more amazing the entire process becomes.

It can also happen that one memory triggers a flood of memories. We call this a "cascade," when information rushes by so fast, you can consciously no longer keep up. This is an amazing energy experience, and when this happens, please enter the cascade experience itself as a Star Event in your Book of Stars, with your current date and age, for example: "The Party Cascade!"

Stepping Inside A Star Memory

Memories flash fast, and often way too fast for the Conscious Mind to keep up, which is used to s-l-o-w, l-i-n-e-a-r language.

To really extract the energy and the information from a Star Memory, we take the time to step inside the memory, and remember more.

This is easy and natural with the high positive memories, and we use the SuperMind process known as the "Classic Game."

Let's think about your Star Memory.

1. Assume the Heart Position.

The Heart Position tells our dear Energy Mind (aka the brain or neurology of your energy body), the Conscious Mind, the physical body and all else who are listening, that we are now going to do something that involves everybody.

The Heart Position also centres you, grounds you, and holds you safe during these adventures in time and space.

- Point to the place on your chest where you would point to say, "This is me!"

- Place the centre of the palm of your leading hand over that spot.

- Place the other hand on top.

- Take a deep breath in and out.

Congratulations! You've learned the Modern Energy Heart Position, a key ingredient to involve the Energy Mind and the Energy Body in our doings, and the start to almost everything we do in Modern Energy.

2. *Think about your Star Memory.*

A tip: If you find it hard to concentrate on your own high positive memory, you are too stressed, which means you are too low in energy, and you need to raise energy first.

There is a list of reliable, quick energy raising techniques in the addendum to refer to if you are new to Modern Energy.

Now, answer the following questions out aloud.

- **In your Star Memory, what did you see?**

Describe the main components (the environment, the landscape, what else was there) out aloud.

Gesture towards things as you talk - "The sun was high in the sky" - point to where the sun was, for example.

Take your time and describe it clearly, as though you were helping another person see what you did see.

Next, we ask:

- **In your Star Memory, what did you hear?**

Tell it out aloud, as though you were helping another person hear what you did hear.

Gesture and point to the sources of the sounds to engage the physical body and the energy body as much as possible.

Now, we ask:

- **In your Star Memory, what did you feel?**

These are the strictly physical sensations, for example, the sand under your bare feet, or the wind in your hair, the sun on your skin.

Make movements to indicate where these physical feelings were experienced, and explain what you experienced as though you were trying to make another person feel what you did feel.

Then, we ask:

- **In your Star Memory, what did you scent?**

That is now the fourth sense we are adding to the experience of the memory. With every sense added, more information and energy begins to flow, and the more real the memory becomes.

Next, we ask:

- **In your Star Memory, what did you taste?**

Moisten your lips, make a smacking sound with your mouth to activate the 5th Sense and add its information and energy to the memory party.

And finally, the 6th Sense:

- **In your Star Memory, how did you feel inside?**

Point to the locations and movements of the energy feelings, the emotions you physically felt at that time.

Take your time, breathe deeply and enjoy exploring your Star Memory in this specific way.

Note how much more information and energy you have discovered in this one memory that flashed by so fast before.

Now, we can also ask questions about this memory.

- Why is this specific memory relevant and important for you to visit today?

- What did the past aspect (the "you" that was then) learn from this experience?

- How did this experience change the aspects life?

- What did you, here and now, discover about this memory that you had not realised before?

- Would you like to have many, many more such amazing experiences in the future?

I invite you to start asking your own questions about your Star Memories.

The Conscious Mind needs to have its questions answered.

The Star Memories are there, they are our proverbial "million dollars in the bank of life."

When we ask questions, we create lines of communication, channels through which essential information and energy then can travel, and we become energy richer, which means more powerful, but we also become wiser.

Important Note: I am 100% convinced that by giving deep attention to our Star Memories, we are telling our totality that we want to experience MORE STAR EVENTS in the future.

We are setting a new direction for all our systems which may have falsely believed that we are only interested in trauma – our own, and that of others.

Setting our direction towards Star Events instead causes a structural change in thinking.

I call this **Star Matrix Thinking**.

The beginning for this course correction is right here.

The more attention you give to your own Star Memories, the more profound these positives changes become.

Helping Other People Recover Star Memories

When we direct attention towards happy memories, people immediately get happier.

In Modern Energy language, they become energy richer.

They rise up on the Modern Energy Chart.

This makes them more attractive to us, more interesting, more loveable.

This is particularly useful with friends and relatives, and being able to make that happen is one of the best side effects of Star Matrix thinking.

I'll pass the microphone to a Star Matrix student, who tells the following story.

> "My mother-in-law is in an old people's home and dutifully, we have to visit once a week. For ten years, I've been dreading those visits. We would arrive, and for an hour or so we would be deluged with all manner of illnesses and misery, and who said what to whom, it was awful and left me, my husband and the kids (who refused to come along eventually, and who could blame them!) totally drained and near suicidal.
>
> "That is until I started the Star Matrix course! After the very first Unit, I walked in, said "Hi!" and my attention fell on one of the many photographs on her bedside table. It showed her with her long dead husband, smiling, standing in front of an old car, in black and white.
>
> "I gave it to her and said, "Tell me about this!" and she told the story of their first new car, they had worked hard, and went to pick it up from the factory, and it was really interesting! She came to life and told other happy stories she remembered. The time just flew by! My husband was totally astonished, and ever since, we've been looking forward to the visits. I just wish we'd known about this ten years ago!"

As a side note, the old lady now has her own Book of Stars, and not only is she much happier, the other people in the old people's home have started sharing their Star Memories among themselves, and with their carers, and the whole place is happier than it was before.

As another side note, the old lady also reported she was amazed at the clarity of her memories, and found other things much easier to remember too, such as dates of birthdays and when appointments were booked.

This does not surprise me. Memory is like so many things a practised art, and we simply get better at things we do more often. With the incentive of getting good emotions, really feeling that resonance of the happy feelings in the past, or as we call it, "connecting with the aspects and their energy," to practice remembering good memories is a win-win for everyone involved.

We should also not underestimate the effects that a happier energy body has on everyone's situations, no matter who they are or what they do.

Recent studies in how chronic pain is processed in the brain showed that when a person is emotionally negative, the experience of pain becomes more severe and causes more reactions in the physical brain.

When a person is emotionally neutral, the experience of pain lessens.

Of course, these studies never even considered making the trial subjects HAPPY as the third point of reference in that scale (see (r)Evolution for my passionate speech on that subject!) but we can plot the trajectory there.

Unhappy people are in more pain than neutral people. Happy people are in less pain. It makes sense that the happier you are, the greater the "pain relieving" effect will become. It's a simple equation we are looking at here.

The old lady in the nursing home was happier now that she had her Star Memories to work with. Happier people also have better immune system functioning, heal faster, have better digestion, to mention just a few.

And I don't even want to start at the social effects of being happier and far more likeable, more attractive, on the fellow inmates and the staff of a nursing home. Or a hospital. Or a prison. Or a school. Or an office, or a sales team …

Being more energy rich is a fine thing, a life changing thing.

To not only make people more energy high for a moment or two, but to actually raise people's energy average, is the core direction of Modern Energy.

Simply re-connecting people with their own long lost Treasures & Riches, their own Star Memories, is such a simple, quick and easy pathway to having more energy rich people in your life, it's quite astonishing.

All you have to do is to direct people's attention to positive events in their lives.

You can just ask them.

"What's the best thing that happened to you last week? Last month? Last year?"

You can use any artefact or physical object a person has on them or in their home as an entry point to high positive memories, because people quite naturally only surround themselves with personal mementos that remind them of something good.

"Tell me about this picture! This vase! This pendant! This ring you are wearing! This tie!"

You can use clearly beloved topics and beings and everything else a person is into as the gateway to an energy raising communication.

"Tell me about your cat! About this car! About your garden! About the music you are playing!"

If you start looking for entry points, portals, into people's positive memories, you will find them all of a sudden absolutely everywhere.

You will never, ever have to be afraid of getting stuck in a lift with a boring person, ever again.

Or being stuck with someone for 12 hours on an air plane.

Or dread having to visit a boring or negative relative, or attending a dreary or confrontational family event.

People become walking bags of Treasures & Riches instead – and somewhere in there may just be the information and the energy YOU need for your own personal evolution.

- **Star Stories have the power to teach us many things, and they have the power to evolve us.**

That's because they are so energy rich, so information dense, and because our Star Stories are the natural way in which human beings pass on their life's wisdom from one to the other.

The Star Inside The Star Memory: The MOMENT

Once we have recovered a few Star Memories and told the Star Story, we begin to notice that there is a reliable structure to our Star Memories, which works as follows.

1. There is a time and place where the aspect is about to have the experience. When we tell the story, this sets the scene for others, and takes us to the Star Memory ourselves.

2. The actual EVENT that happens inside the aspect's energy system is actually very short – it is just a MOMENT. The MOMENT of enlightenment, that lightning strike through the energy system that catapults the aspect up to a different level altogether.

3. After the event, there is what I call an afterglow as the aspect experiences the world in a whole new way.

The Star Aspect is the one that is having their MOMENT of revelation; this is the "Star" that is one of the Stars in your Star Matrix.

When we interact with our own or other people's Star Memories, we want to pay particular attention to that MOMENT, the moment the "Star was born," the moment of enlightenment.

The best, highest and most powerful energy experiences are right there in that moment.

The most information and inspiration is right there, in that moment.

By focusing on the moment inside the whole Star Story, we learn and understand that what we are seeking in the future is likewise, not great long stretches of times of happiness, but that we are on a quest for those Star MOMENTS that change everything, and which are the markers of our personal evolution.

For practice, go to your Book of Stars and pick three Star Memories to discover the Star Moment within the Star Story.

Discovering Different Perspectives

Star Memories are great for practising how to explore memories in general in more detail, and therefore being able to gain more insights, information, and energy.

We can take different standpoints in our Star Memories.

1. We can experience from a distance what the aspect did in the memory habitat by telling the story of the aspect's experience in past tense.

2. We can make the experiences of the aspect more current and more relevant by telling the story of the aspect in present tense.

3. We can get a resonant experience by telling the story in past tense, first person.

4. We can get a high energy experience by telling the story in present tense, first person.

Try this out with a Star Memory of your own, and remember to speak out aloud.

1. Aspect, Past Tense

A three year old aspect was on holiday with her parents. They went to the beach together and there, pony rides along the sands were offered. Father put the aspect on a brown and white pony, and mother and father walked alongside the aspect. The aspect was blissfully happy.

2. Aspect, Present Tense

The three year old aspect is on holiday with her parents, and they arrive on the beach. The aspect spots ponies and begs to be allowed to ride. The father agrees and chooses a brown and white pony. The father lifts up the aspect, puts her on the pony, and mother and father walk alongside the aspect, keeping her steady on the pony, down the white sandy beach.

3. Inhabiting the Aspect, Past Tense

I was three years old and went on holiday with my parents. We went to the beach, and I spotted ponies to ride! My dad gave the man some money, lifted me up on the pony, and my mum and dad walked alongside as I was riding the pony on the beach. I don't think I've ever been so happy.

4. Inhabiting the Aspect, Present Tense

I am three years old and I am on holiday with my parents. It is early morning and we are going to the beach! I'm so excited! There is the big blue sea and the white sands, the sun is shining and sparkling on the sea, and then I see the ponies! I LOVE ponies! Please, please can I ride the pony? My dad is laughing and gives the man some money, I choose the brown and white pony with the long white tail, and he lifts me up, and I am riding a pony!!! My mum and dad are either side and I'm not afraid now, this is the best thing that's ever happened to me! I could ride forever on the white sand by the blue sea with mum and dad by my side, keeping me safe.

Important Note: Don't be put off by the grammar words, past tense, present tense.

The fact that we can change our stand point in a memory, and inhabit our aspects if we choose to do this, is a fantastic skill that everyone has.

The language we use helps us take the position we want to take, and when we start to tell the story out aloud, the attitude of consciousness happens easily and automatically.

Please note that these four ways to reconnect with a memory are not better or worse than each other. They are different. Different things are learned and experienced from these different stand points.

When we want to directly connect with the aspect in the memory, we can do this by stepping inside the memory and interacting directly with the aspect.

For example:

> The aspect is riding along the beach and I, as I am here and now, position myself halfway along the path between the start and the turning point. As the little aspect rides by, I can see that she is wearing a black safety hat that is quite a bit too big for her and she has to put her head back to be able to see; but she is holding the reins well and has the biggest smile on her face. I wave to the little girl on the horse, and she turns to look at me but doesn't let go of the reins. And then the mother waves back to me!

Our marvellous minds can do such wonderful things for us.

Our amazing Conscious Mind is a true Time-Space-Ship that can travel freely anytime, anywhere.

It can provide us with experiences that make the energy body react powerfully – that is why we can laugh and cry, and laugh again in story or a play.

The ability of our amazing Conscious Minds to do that, to affect the energy body so profoundly regardless of what is actually happening in the physical world, or in the Hard, is an enormous gift for life.

Our Energy Bodies are the very foundation of all we think, of all we believe, of all we feel, and everything we do.

Our Energy Bodies create our emotions, all of them, all the time. Our Energy Bodies decide if we are stupid, or intelligent; if we act with wisdom and with grace, or stumble around our various incarnations like a bunch of fools.

Star Memories are the easiest, quickest and cheapest way to raise energy fast, to make the Energy Body feel good, and to connect ourselves directly to aspects who were extremely powerful, known to mankind thus far.

While we are here, let me explain a foundational thought model from Modern Energy.

The Three Planes

Most people in the Western World have been brought up to believe that there is nothing beyond a material universe. This is … sad, to say the least; a catastrophe for humanity, as I like to think of it.

So, we have a physical reality.

This is also known as "nature," and goes all the way from the smallest pond scum all the way to the stars in the sky, and everything in between.

Physical reality is very orderly and highly structural. It is also very predictable, and very reliable. There is the kind of cause and effect here that we human beings can understand – naturally.

Then, we have the energy worlds, or the Oceans of Energy, as I like to call them.

This is a non-material plane, where everything is made of energy, and where different rules of nature apply. The energy realms also have beautiful rules and regulations, which are also reliable, although sometimes very different from the rules of the physical plane.

But then, we have what I call "the Hard."

I don't call it the Hard because it's hard, but because it is so hard to live there.

This is what human beings have constructed in all their various doings. It's the Universe of man-made objects and things, and the Universe of man made religions, laws, philosophies, societal constructs, thought models, language and all and everything the human children have made.

The Hard sits between physical reality and the energy worlds, and it is exempt from the natural laws that guide everything else. For example, if you plant a tree and do everything right, it will grow, produce apples, and you have your just reward for your labours. In the Hard, you can do everything right, and might still end up in prison or on the scaffold, entirely unjustly, entirely in contradiction to all that is right, or true, or holy.

The Hard is that confusing fog in the human equations, and once we clearly understand that the Hard is man-made (human-made!), and therefore, we can change it, as we are also humans, the exact type that made the Hard as it is today, a lot of stress and confusion simply evaporates.

Here is the Three Levels Energy-Meditation to help us internalise dealing with these three layers that together, ARE the reality we find ourselves in.

The Three Levels Energy Meditation

1. Assume the Heart Position. Look down at yourself. Breathe in deeply and become aware of your physical body. Tap your hands on your chest, lightly. Stamp your feet on the floor. This is physical reality.

2. Stay in the Heart Position and look straight ahead. Now you can become aware of all the objects in your environment, the visible ones as well as all the laws that govern your life invisibly, the taxes you pay, the societal structures that shape your life – this is the Hard, the Universe of man made things, the second layer.

3. Stay in the Heart Position and raise your eyes up high. Keep breathing deeply. Let your wonderful Conscious Mind take you up, through the roof of your dwelling, up, up above the clouds, up above the atmosphere, higher still – this is the realm where the Stars live, the energy worlds, where we are pure consciousness and everything is made of energy.

This is the realm where your Star Memories are – high, high above the grey of every day, and this is the space where we will form our Star Matrix, a self concept constructed only from the highest Star Memories of your very own life.

I encourage you strongly to use the 3 Levels Meditation any time you want to start doing something special with your Star Memories, to get you in the right frame of mind, and to let our Mind/Body/Spirit Totality know that we are going to be working in that energy space, because that is where your Star Memories are.

Collecting More Star Memories

Now, it's over to you and YOUR Star Memories. Unusually, this book is not about teaching you what I know, but what you know! A delicious proposition and as with all things, practice makes you get much better at this, and the more you practice, the easier the Star Memories come to you.

I am going to personally encourage you to start adding as many entries in your Book of Stars as you can.

I am going to suggest that you look through your entries to find a Star Memory that you feel highly inspired to engage with more deeply.

You might want to re-experience the Star Memory, using the No. 4 pattern and becoming one with the aspect, re-experiencing what the aspect did experience. You might want to touch and exchange energy with the aspect, or just observe the aspect quietly from a distance.

The beautiful thing is that these are YOUR Star Memories, and YOU get to do with them 100% what YOU want to do with them.

- **Let your fascinations be your guide!**

Your fascinations are your compass that guides you in the worlds of energy to that which is really important to you, important for you, and will help you grow, become more powerful and help you move on to the next level in this lifetime.

Collect Star Memories in your Book of Stars until you have at least 100 entries. Star Memory recovery is exponential. This means that the first 3 or 4 might require really thinking about it, but then, they come faster; and every person has their own number where a threshold shift occurs, and all of a sudden, all the Star Memories are accessible at will.

You can also expect surprises along the way!

When I was creating the Star Matrix Masters course, I also took part in it and did all the exercises. The inaugural course began on November 11th, 2019, so we were about four units in, when Christmas happened, as it does in the Hard.

I found myself at a party which also included my ex-husband. We have been divorced for a long time, but we had been married for 25 years and there are predictable patterns between us, real rail road tracks of conversations that were always bordering on an argument that could never be resolved.

Very predictable, very tedious, and beyond tiring after all those years ...

Yes, and so it started out on the old railroad to the old arguments, but then, all of a sudden and completely unexpectedly, completely unasked for, my dear, dear Energy Mind flashed me up a memory of the ex-husband, standing at the photocopier all night long, helping to produce a newsletter for the club my aspect was running at the time. Wow. I had not thought of that in decades.

I stopped the conversational track we were on, and I said to the ex, "You know, I don't think I ever thanked you for all the help you gave me when I first started out. You stood all night at the photocopier, even though you had to go to work at 7am the next day, and I was too busy back then to appreciate that properly, or to say, THANK YOU."

The change in atmosphere, not just between me and the ex, but in the entire room, was astonishing. It literally was as though a switch had been flipped. The ex looked at me with utter astonishment, then cleared his throat and said, "Yes, I remember that. I was always glad to help."

The very next day, he came to my house with the gift of a band saw, and we haven't bickered since.

I immediately reported this astonishing experience to the Star Matrix student's group, and this is when I used the term "Star Matrix Thinking" for the first time.

To be fair, I have no idea what my aspect at that party was thinking, or whether she was even thinking at all, on that old, long, long entrained bickering train track with the ex. But the memory of the ex, standing at the photocopier at 3am in the morning, and then the decision to give voice to that, and to thank him, that was a new way of thinking I had never experienced before in this context.

This is just one example of the "surprises" that await us when we start thinking differently about ourselves, about our lives, and finally pay the long overdue attention to the high positive memories. I know, have known for a long time, that going to positive memories for inspiration and guidance is the right thing to do. I also knew that this would have to change the way we think about the world. However, I did not expect so many positive, beneficial, every day surprises.

You will experience them too.

Star Matrix induced Star Experiences will await you too in your future.

Just make sure you become a real treasure hunter, make this your new favourite hobby, and it all starts with the Treasures & Riches we have already accumulated in this lifetime.

The Conscious Mind & The Energy Mind

The Conscious Mind and the Energy Mind are really a single system (the **SuperMind!**) and they are supposed to work together seamlessly.

When we are energy high, they do; and the lower we go on the Modern Energy Chart, or the more stressed we become, the more they split apart and fail to communicate with one another.

"Communication" means a flow of energy and information; and so it makes sense that when we are energy rich, and lots of energy flows easily around our systems, we gain access to more energy AND more information, at the same time.

That makes everyone happier and we are in a lovely upward lifting spiral of unfoldment.

When we are engaging with our own memories, this gives us two tips.

It becomes easier and easier to access memories, the higher we are on the Modern Energy Chart.

So to make "Star Memory Recovery" easier, we raise energy before we start.

However, the very attempt to think about a high positive memory, a Star Memory, raises energy all by itself and without further ado.

As soon as the memory appears, we connect with those higher energy states and that raises our energy in the Here & Now.

This is great news, because it gives us a fantastic, bullet proof method of raising energy in ourselves at any time, anywhere, for the price of a thought – and to raise other people's energy fast, reliably, quickly, and without even having to mention a single thing about energy, Conscious Minds or Energy Minds, for that matter.

I do believe that when we are consciously clear on what we are doing, everything works so much better, and having a great relationship between the Conscious Mind and the Energy Mind is not just fantastic for Star Matrix, it is a gift for life that keeps on giving.

Dear Energy Mind!

Everything I've ever heard and read about the "unConscious Mind" or worse still, the "subConscious Mind" was just so hopelessly convoluted and downright wrong, it made me want to weep.

I knew from an entire lifetime of experience that the mysterious side of us that would send inspirations, dreams, insights and real life life-saving warnings was 100% on our side, that it was the very key to the greatest wonders and mysteries of the multiverse, and I loved it with all my heart.

When I was creating a conceptual framework for the real, living energy body which everybody has, whether they like it or not, whether they know it or not, or whether they strenuously deny it, or not, I came up with the idea to say that the energy body is not a collection of skimpy needly lines, a billion dots, chakras stacked up like dinner plates, a mysterious onion with all these astral layers, or a mush-mash of all of the Chinese whispers of the ages, or subtle in any way – but in fact, it's a real LIVING BODY.

A real body, that is hungry and thirsty – but not for food and water, for ENERGY instead.

The living energy body takes in energy for food, and lets energy go that's not used. It breathes and drinks energy in, through, and out.

When this real energy body gets hurt, it has real energy wounds, and those real energy wounds need real energy healing – obviously!

When the energy body is happy, it sends us cries of joy through our emotions; and when it's unhappy, it sends us cries of pain instead.

The energy body is direct, and simple. When the energy injury is in the energy stomach, that's where we feel the emotions; when the energy injury is in the head, that's where we feel the emotions. 100% reasonable, rational, and reliable.

Our real living energy body has an energy heart, and energy hands, energy feet too, and it has a head! And that head is our **dear Energy Mind.**

As all things in the real living energy body, our dear Energy Mind deals with ENERGY. It knows about energy, it understands energy, it works with energy, it is made from energy.

The Energy Mind is our full on connection to the Oceans of Energy; it is our guide and specialist on understanding energy, working with energy, and navigating safely and confidently in the energy worlds.

So this is why I call the Energy Mind the Energy Mind, to totally step away from all previous entrainments, insanities, disrespects, and the nonsense of the ages, and give us a fresh start to explore what our dear Energy Minds have to offer, when we treat them right, respect them, and start to learn their amazing ways.

Every relationship works better when there is more love flowing between the partners; and love is just another word for energy, and information, so we really start with thinking of our own energy minds not just as any old energy minds, but our very own DEAR Energy Minds.

Now I have found, and this is really highly amusing in its perfection and simplicity, that the way the Conscious Mind and the Energy Mind start to work together best for the beginner is to give this simple rule:

- **The Conscious Mind asks the question, and the Energy Mind provides the answer.**

I want you to think of this as an actual two-way conversation.

The Conscious Mind asks a question.

Now, the Conscious Mind has to STOP, and switch into RECEIVING MODE, just as you would in any conversation, phone conversation, radio conversation, to give the other party a chance to answer.

If you find this difficult to conceptualise, try the following exercise.

The Phone Exercise

Pick up your phone and hold it to your ear. Ask a question out aloud, such as, "What is my favourite memory relating to water?"

Now you will naturally switch from question mode into receiving mode; you listen/wait for the answer.

Does a memory come to you?

Have you remembered something relating to water?

If you did, now you need to complete that conversation. You don't just put the phone away when someone has been helpful and answered your question.

- **Now we say out aloud, "Thank you, dear Energy Mind!"**

Why is that important?

Well, consciously, to all of us living in lamentably low energy states almost all of the time, the dear Energy Mind is an alien, a stranger, of whom we personally know next to nothing.

We have no idea of its actual powers, and some among us are nervous or afraid of this entity we are sharing our lives with, and which has been accused of all sorts of malfeasance by people who had no idea what or whom they were actually talking about.

Some people have been told that the Energy Mind is some kind of superbeing that is oh! so much smarter and cleverer than "we" are and we need to consciously grovel to it in some way.

Other people have been told that it's the repository of all things evil and it's out to get us, sabotage us, is our enemy and we're better off without it altogether.

We need to leave all of that behind. Our dear, dear Energy Minds are ours, just as our hands are our hands, and our feet are our feet.

They want us to thrive, they want us to be the happiest we can possibly be and will fight for us to the bitter end, just as every single cell in our physical bodies will fight for us, all the way, unconditionally, and without fail.

- **Our Energy Minds love us unconditionally.**

This we need to re-learn, really understand, and by being loving and respectful to our dear Energy Minds, we start a new relationship, perhaps the most important relationship any of us will ever know, and one that will pay dividends, not just in this life, but also in the afterlife.

It is our dear Energy Minds who "send us the memories."

When we start with Star Matrix, it is the Energy Mind who decides which memories to send us.

The Energy Mind might not understand many of the strange and convoluted, stress riddled doings of human beings and the Hard, but the Energy Mind does understand energy, and it is pretty much the only entity we have direct access to right now, who knows the actual conditions of your own energy body inside and out, and across your lifetime, at that.

- **When we ask for a Star Memory, the dear Energy Mind will send us the one out of a myriad of possible memories that is suitable and RIGHT for you, right here and now.**

When you have only one or two memories, or even ten or twenty, the complex, multidimensional structure, order and sequence of these memories is not apparent to the Conscious Mind.

Why is the Energy Mind sending me memories about eating candyfloss at a fun fair, that time my boss said the report was the best he'd ever seen, when that nice lady gave me change for the bus home that night, that time I got drunk and swam naked in a lake???

Here, I have to ask you to trust your dear Energy Mind to know what's right, and what's best.

- **The Energy Mind – YOUR dear Energy Mind! - is the expert on YOUR energy system.**

Consciously, we literally have no idea what's going on with our multidimensional energy bodies here and now, and never mind in the context of prelife and afterlife soul progressions and all of that. But we can learn. We have these amazing brains, and we can make new connections, through which more energy and information will flow, and when enough information has been assembled, there is a threshold shift. The Conscious Mind has its Aha! Moment, or even Eureka!!! and the connections have become apparent.

Every time that happens, our faith and trust, as well as our amazement and LOVE for our dear Energy Minds take a leap upward, and we have literally evolved as human beings in mind, body and spirit.

So here, in Star Matrix, we start our relationship with our dear Energy Mind and our dear Conscious Mind by simply following this pattern.

1. Assume the Heart Position. That's the sign for our totality we are going to do something that involves everyone. It switches on the whole person.

2. Ask the dear Energy mind a question, or make a request, using the phrasing, "Dear Energy Mind! PLEASE give me ... (a Star Memory that is perfect for me today!)."

3. Switch to receiving mode; just keep breathing deeply in the Heart Position and await the response. You don't have to do anything further consciously now.

4. A memory will flash up.

5. Once you "know" what it is, say a heartfelt, "Wow, thank you, dear Energy Mind!"

This simple, basic pattern now opens the door to receive Star Memories that are relevant, important, and the exact right energy and information you need, right here and now, to make you happier, to make you stronger, to learn more and to help you evolve as a person.

Practise this.

The rewards will be far more than you ever expected.

The Power Of Inspiration

What is inspiration? Well, it's the proverbial lightning strike that makes a person jump up, shout, "Eureka!" and dance in the streets – and then go into action and DO something amazing, something new, something in a whole new way.

The fun part about this is that when we consider the world on the other side of the Modern Energy paradigm shift, where we all have real living energy bodies, and we calculate reality with six senses, and not just five, "inspiration" ceases to be a mystical inexplicable lightning strike, and become an obvious, natural process instead.

Inspiration is a natural process we can encourage and facilitate.

Inspiration happens when in a person's energy body a final connection is made, and more energy and information all of sudden flows through the system, bringing with it insights, the bigger picture and at the same time, the physical energy to DO something about it.

Would it surprise you if I told you that our own Star Memories are the most direct and greatest source of inspiration we can access, right here and now?

We don't need to find the next inspirational speaker to get the exact right inspiration for whatever it is we are trying to achieve – right here, right now.

The reason for this being so is that our life experiences are not disconnected, isolated, random events.

There is a theme, a story, a journey there.

Our Star Memories are dots that want to be connected.

When that happens, not only do we get the path we've travelled so far, but we also gain the trajectory – the road into the future.

That's one of my favourite words – trajectory.

We really do have a path, each one us, in the pathless land in which we all travel.

Our Star Memories are milestones on this path.

First, we discover them.

Then we can use them to gain power, to gain speed, to overcome obstacles, blockages and reversals, and as a source of not just true inspiration, but the EXACT RIGHT INSPIRATION we need in that exact moment.

That is so groovy, I can't think of another word for it.

And it's easy.

Especially if our dear, dear Energy Minds are finally on board!

Our Own Star Stories Of Inspiration

There was a salesman who was struggling in the changing, stressful economy. He asked his dear Energy Mind for sales inspiration, and got the memory of a young aspect, selling records from the boot of his mother's car at a country faire. The sheer joy of selling, the bright sunshine, the happy customers and the overflowing box of money gave him the boost and the exact right attitude he needed to go forward right then.

There was an artist who was struggling with selling her art. She asked her dear Energy Mind for a Star Memory that would help her on one particularly dreary day, where once again, nobody had bought her art. Her Energy Mind sent her the memory of having done a painting as a very young aspect, rushing to show her parents, and there was a visitor on that day, and he loved the painting so much, he offered to buy it for five dollars, as he wanted to hang it up in his office to cheer him up on dreary days. The artist realised that she had lost the sheer joy of her art somewhere along the way, trying to do things to please people, rather than that fabulous, pure love of colours and creating that the young aspect had experienced, and started a brand new line of paintings there and then – and those paintings actually SOLD.

There was a lady who was totally frustrated with her husband's untidiness and total refusal to do any housework at all, or even clean up after himself in the slightest. She asked her dear Energy Mind for a Star Memory that could help in any way with this everlasting problem that was ruining their relationship. The memory she got was of her aspect who was about 12 years old, and who had grown tired of piles of books falling over in her bedroom in her parent's house. The aspect had found an old bookcase in the cellar, dragged it up the stairs, and arranged her beloved books in alphabetical order according to title on it. In the Star Memory, the aspect was looking at the beautifully ordered bookshelf with the marvellous books in it, standing like a beacon of light, order, beauty and excitement in a sea of discarded clothes, magazines, shoes and all sorts of debris, and not soon after, her entire bedroom was beautiful and tidy. She realised that she could start with books and a bookshelf for her husband too, that *he had missed out such an experience when he was young*, and decided to encourage him to build a book case to order and sort his own books. This was the beginning of a journey that was mutually satisfying for both, and the end to the endless complaining and shouting, which had never gotten her anywhere at all.

What are the intractable problems in your life, the ones you are struggling with every day, right here and now?

What could happen if your dear Energy Mind sent you a memory of something that not someone else had done, achieved or experienced, but that YOU did do, that YOU did achieve, that YOU did experience?

This is a beautiful thing.

This is starting to make use of the proverbial Treasures & Riches that each one carries with us, unbeknownst to us, unexplored, un-activated.

I love this process so very much.

It's not just the power of personal inspiration; it is also that process of learning just what our dear Energy Minds can do for us, if we ask nicely.

I would like to make the important note that to ask the dear Energy Mind for Star Memories that contain inspiration and information you need right now isn't the end of the game.

Once we have asked a few times, received an answer, acted on it and thanked our dear, dear Energy Mind for this amazing gift, the process itself takes on a life of its own.

The dear Energy Mind becomes encouraged to send us positive memories to help us out in every day life.

Do you remember the story of me and my ex at the Christmas party? I wasn't meditating, I was right in the middle of real life unfolding, getting frustrated, and my dear, dear Energy Mind sent me the memory of the ex-husband standing in front of the photocopier at 3am without me having asked for it. That is a real gift.

This has happened in various ways many times since then, and it's surprising, beautiful, and turns situations around on a dime that could otherwise have been difficult, painful or boring.

We are creating brand new lines of high energy, positive communication when we practise Star Matrix – and the more you use these lines of communication, especially at the start, the more energy, information and INSPIRATION for new action is then available to you.

Now, it's over to you.

Pick a problem you have, right here, right now.

Ask your dear Energy Mind for a Star Memory that can help you with this.

> *"Dear Energy Mind! Please give me a Star Memory that can help me with my problem with ..."*

Get the memory. Make the connections.

And remember to enter this memory in your Book of Stars!

(There is much more energy and information in this memory than you already understood; this memory is one of the dots that will help you find your trajectory!)

A Star Is A Star ... Is A Star ...

On the very first Star Matrix course, there was a participant who kept insisting that they could not find any Star Memories.

When we explored this further, it turned out that this person was trying to find major enlightenment events and kept rejecting the memories their dear Energy Mind was actually sending them as "not good enough."

For example, when this person asked for a Star Memory, their Energy Mind sent a memory of a young teenage aspect, having bunked off school and having fun with friends by a fountain in the town centre.

The person immediately rejected this memory as being irrelevant to all their hideous, serious problems of the day, not meaningful, and just "random nonsense."

From the outside, it is immediately clear what the problem is here. The Energy Mind was holding up a sign saying, "You're too serious, you need to take time off your problems and have some fun with other people, lighten up!"

From this, I came up with the concept that "A Star is a Star!"

It doesn't matter if the Star Memory your dear Energy Mind sends you is just a short moment of happiness in the most mundane of circumstances, or some massive earth-shaking incidence of true enlightenment.

A Star is a Star!

We need to learn to say, "Thank you, dear Energy Mind!" and at the very least faithfully tell the Star Story out aloud, and then enter it into our Book of Stars.

I do understand that many of us, if not all of us, have acquired all sorts of shields and protective devices against "teachers and gurus" over our lifetimes, and that's a very good thing indeed. It keeps us safe.

But our own dear Energy Minds are NOT parents, teachers, priests or other forms of authorities who want to make us into something we're not.

In the contrary.

Our dear Energy Minds are 100% on our side, they are us!

We can listen to them in the same way we can listen to our own beating hearts, and know they're doing the best they can for us.

So in return, we need to respect them and receive them without prejudice.

Once, when visiting a very old person, my mother gave me an excellent piece of advice that has stood me in good stead ever since.

She said, "This old person will want to give you something. They're a bit crazy, but don't take any notice of what it is. Just take it, say Thank You! And you can always throw it away later, it's not a problem."

And right on! The old person decided to give me a crate of onions they had grown in their garden, and my aspect was around 14 years old at the time – the onions could not have been more irrelevant to her at that time if they tried! But she heeded her mother's advice, thanked them for the gift of the onions, and the old person was much pleased by this, and added an odd looking vase as an additional gift on top.

In the car on the way home, my mother said the onions were great, she'd take them and use them for cooking, and my aspect kept the odd looking vase, sort of as a reminder of having understood the principle that when someone offers you a gift, please just take it and say Thank You! You can always throw it away later.

As I write this, and reflect on it further, I realise that the Onion Story is actually a Star Story. I remember with absolute brilliant clarity the old person with that box of onions, and the sunrise smile on their face when I said, "Yes, thank you!" and held out my hands to receive them.

I realise that this principle, of taking things unconditionally when offered (because you can always throw them away later if you want, it's safe to do that!) has stood me in such good stead, but also, it goes far beyond just taking material objects.

"Taking these gifts that are offered" in their widest metaphorical sense extends to information, to love, to all manner of things, rippling out, so far, so wide!

I'm having a Star Matrix moment here whilst writing this book!

Perhaps my Star Story of the Onion Gift (inscribed in my Book of Stars, 1973, age 14!) can help you understand how the dear Energy Mind feels when we receive the gift they have given us. It's really a wonderful, very loving thing to do.

As the onions turned out to be so useful to my mother, and the odd vase became an artefact for the aspect, we don't really know at the point where the gift of the Star Memory is given, if it's going to be useful or not. We have to receive it first in order to find that out!

So please, whatever positive memory your dear Energy Mind sends, don't judge it for being faulty, or irrelevant, or useless, or "not starry enough." Don't reject it. Accept it and it will open new lines of enquiry, new channels of communication.

In that context, there's something else I noticed.

The first newly recovered Star Memories are not the most amazing ones. It's like the dear Energy Mind sends us memories we can consciously cope with at first. Easy, simple, and direct.

As we do more of it, we discover more deep and very powerful Star Memories.

These first gifts are not all there is. As my 20 year old aspect discovered when they found out that the old onion person had left them 10,000 Deutschmarks in their will. Which was exactly enough for a deposit on a small house in England at that time.

Wow.

Star Dreams

What if the Star Experience didn't happen in physical reality at all?

What if it "just" happened ...

- in a dream
- in meditation
- in Sanctuary
- with the aid of drugs
- whilst reading a book
- as the result of an intellectual breakthrough
- whilst listening to someone else's Star Story
- in your imagination???

Surely, such memories don't count, because they were not hard enough, and there is no physical evidence, such as eye witnesses, photographs or surveillance videos to show that it was real?

Ah, but you see, A Star is A Star.

It doesn't matter where it came from, or how it came into being.

There are all sorts of high positive memories of Star Events that have little or no physical component at all, and some have an extra physical component, such as a shamanic drug, and none of that matters.

The only thing that matters is that YOU know exactly how powerful that experience was for your aspect at the time, still is, for you right now, and that this is a true Star Event for you.

- **I call the non-physical Star Events the Star Dreams.**

One of my very earliest Star Memories was indeed, a dream. It was perfectly lucid but at the same time, clearly magical in nature. A very young aspect, 2 years old perhaps, walked into the cellar of the home in her dream. The store room was completely empty – apart from a table right in the centre, on which an amazing array of magical toys that sparkled in all the colours of the rainbow awaited her. The aspect knew and understood that these were HER TOYS. No grown up was handing them out or having to be asked or begged with at all – these were her toys to play with as she pleased.

This Star Dream, this Star Event of "finding the magical toys inside" changed the aspect and the way she did things profoundly and forever. She returned to the toy room many times and it was the beginning of her first Sanctuary, and having access to a parallel life, that was just as real as the Hard, and the presence of which saved her life.

In our societies, fantasy and day dreaming are profoundly discouraged on every level; every child that awakes crying in the night because of a dream that affected their energy system so profoundly, their heart is racing, sweat is pouring from their physical body and they are trembling all over are being told, "It's only a dream .. it's not real ..."

There are many, many other manifestations of this trying to deny the reality of human experiences and instead of finding out more about them, just to pretend it doesn't happen, or it's only for crazy people.

For example, we have been entrained to believe that invisible friends are bad, and the sign of a child too lonely or mentally disturbed to have "real" friends, meaning hard friends.

Invisible friends are real. They have a real effect on the living energy body, and through the energy body, they have a very real effect on all sorts of physical things, including the blood pressure, the blood sugar levels, the various hormones that dance about our physical bodies, what the neurons in our brains are doing, and so much more besides. The invisible friends also have a direct effect on what we think, and all of that together drives actual, REAL behaviour in the Hard.

- **Just because something isn't hard does not mean it isn't real.**

In fact, there are many, many more things in the non-physical universe happening and going on all the time as the poor brainwashed citizens of the Hard will ever know.

Star Dreams that changed us profoundly are among the most amazing Star Events we could ever have.

The Star Dreams absolutely belong in your Book of Stars, rightfully and finally side by side with any happy memories of standing at the altar as a young bride, or holding the firstborn son in your arms.

An Energy Star is A Star …

This brings me to a truly delightful realisation about the Star Events in our lives.

You don't have to be physically fit, young, strong, sexually attractive, rich, well connected, lucky or anything at all in order to have true Star Events, and to have many, many more.

You can have Star Dreams to complete your Star Matrix.

You can have Star Events that are independent of physical circumstances, or what is happening in Hard.

This puts our basic human ability of consciously travelling anywhere in time and space to good use, and allows us to collect many, many more Stars for our Star Matrix before our physical demise.

Here are further examples of Star Dreams to guide you in the right direction.

> During a party that involved psychedelic drugs aplenty, this young man went outside into the night. The stars in the sky were incredibly bright, and they were dancing. The young man felt his spirit detach from his body and travel up to the stars, become one with the stars, and when he returned, he knew that he was more than his physical body.

Please note: If a photograph of the young man had been taken that night, it would show him sitting, eyes closed, on a log, "doing absolutely nothing at all." And yet, he was having a real experience that changed his life forever, and is the very first entry in this gentleman's Book of Stars.

> This lady tells the story of building her first Sanctuary, a nice house with a garden, and roses round the doors. She used to go there before falling asleep at nights and enjoyed it in a fashion. Until one night, as she transferred her consciousness to her Sanctuary, she found that the house was gone completely, the garden had become a veritable Garden of Eden, and there was a beautiful crystalline fountain right in the middle – and she realised that "I am not alone, I really do have an Energy Mind, and it is beautiful, and it loves me."

Another lady has this Star Story:

> A young aspect, 5 years old, sobbing on her bed because her beloved grandmother had died, the only person who had shown any sympathy for her, or understanding, in her entire life. It was getting dark outside, and nobody came to check in on the little girl, or comfort her. She was tired from the crying and very hungry, her head hurt badly, and then, all of a sudden, there was a soft white glow in the room, and there was the grandmother, sitting on a chair by the side of the bed, her hands folded in her lap, smiling, and the little girl felt such peace, such love. Her hunger went away and so did the pain in her head and in her heart, and she understood that although grandmother was in heaven now, she was still loving her, and still there for her, now and forever.

Star Dreams are just wonderful. They are among the most wonderful, life saving experiences a human being can have – and we do have them, every one of us does. It's a human thing.

Star Dreams belong right side by side with all the other star experiences of our lifetimes, and to reconnect our Star Dreams with all the other Star Memories is a wonderful process that will finally let us understand ourselves better – not as worm fodder, biological robots or walking sacks of trauma, but actually, as multidimensional beings right at home in a truly multidimensional Universe.

Now, it's over to you.

- Assume the Heart Position and do the 3 Levels Meditation.

- Ask your dear Energy Mind to remind you of a Star Dream of your own.

- Tell the Star Story out aloud, and then enter it in your Book of Stars.

- Always remember to add further Star Dreams as and when they occur.

- Our purpose here is to set direction towards further Star Dreams in the future.

With every Star Memory we consciously recover and connect, our Star Matrix becomes more clearly defined. The Star Matrix grows and expands. As it does, we begin to change our minds, each one of us, as to who we really are, and what we can really do in this lifetime – and beyond.

Most importantly, the Star Dreams open the door wide to have many, MANY more Star Events in our future, regardless of our physical circumstances, or what's happening in the Hard.

Star Dreams can take us further, and they can also provide any Missing Events that we need to complete and activate our Star Matrix.

Star People

Star People is my term for beings who directly caused a Star Event to happen inside of us.

A Star Person by my definition triggered an evolutionary, positive shift in our own energy systems. Often, this was not their intention, or they were entirely unknowing of this; but that doesn't matter. What matters is what Star People did for us, and that's what puts their name in our Book of Stars.

I consider it to be the highest honour you can pay to another person to inscribe their name in your Book of Stars.

Star People Are Teachers

A Star Event brings with it that we learn something radically new that we never knew before. Our worlds expand, and we can understand more, know more than we did before.

In that sense, all our Star People are teachers for us; and it makes it easy to start finding Star Memories relating to the Star People in our lives.

In the old oriental traditions, there is the concept of the "Golden Line," where a teacher passes precious information to their student, and they in turn pass this on to another student when they become the teacher.

I'd like you to think of this precious information not as a huge and heavy book full of scribbled writings, but instead, of a ball of pure energy and information that changes the student's energy system as it is "built into" the student's energy body, creating new connections through which new energy and information now can flow.

A Star Teacher thereby doesn't just change the student's mind, but changes their energy body, and thereby, their being.

- **A Star Teacher helps us evolve.**

Take a moment now to reflect upon the Star Teachers in your life. Remember, this is not about long stretches of time, but those extra special moments when something catalysed for you, and the the world was never the same again.

Find a Star Moment that happened because of another person and write the name of your first Star Person into your Book of Stars.

Reflect what it was you learned from them. You may also consider if there is a way to pass on this ball of energy and information to other people in some way, or if you have done this already.

We can also then ask for more Star Teachers to be remembered now, and their name to be entered in the Book of Stars.

More Star People …

When we start thinking about our personal Star People, and when we start actively searching for the people who had the most positive impact on our lives, what we find is always very surprising.

Firstly, there are many more than we consciously realised before starting on this exploration.

Secondly, our personal Star People come from anywhere, at any time, and often, we only met with them physically for a brief flashing moment, once, and never again.

- **A person becomes a Star Person because of a Star Event they triggered in our energy bodies.**

Therefore, we can have relationships that last decades, and still that person isn't a Star Person.

Star Matrix and the Book of Stars is only about the Star Events in your life, remembered.

Please take some time and reflect on your Star People.

Enter their names in your Book of Stars, with a short description and explanation why they are there.

This is a great honour, as well as a great way to say THANK YOU to your Star People for helping you evolve.

Star Beings

Not all Star Beings are people.

Animals can be Star Beings in a person's life too, when something happened because of the animal being there, that caused a threshold shift, an evolution.

There is also the possibility of friends from the plant kingdom have caused a threshold shift; be this a tree, a medicinal plant or any other being, if it caused a Star Event for you, this being also belongs into the Book of Stars.

And here, we come to the understanding as before, namely that …

A Star Being Is A Star Being

Just because something isn't hard, that doesn't mean it isn't real.

Star Beings also include invisible friends, angels, powerfully positive helpful spirits, fictional characters, and any other kind of entity that caused us to transform to a higher level.

In Star Matrix, we cease to discriminate between all the Star Beings, and they all belong in our Book of Stars, side by side, without prejudice, because they were important to us, they helped us to evolve, and can be a major source of power and inspiration when we connect with their energy now.

Every one of us has literally innumerable Star Beings who have helped us along the way.

To consciously understand this extraordinary fact (at last) goes a long, long way to re-interpret the meaning of our lives, and our experiences, in a totally different way.

The Star Beings alone are proof positive that we were, indeed loved; that we indeed, received so much help, that we were never alone, that we were and are connected to other beings in an extraordinary network, where beings help each other and catalyse evolution.

You Are A Star Person Too

It is literally impossible to go through life and not also help another entity on their path.

We too have catalysed an evolution in another person, helped them to have a Star Event of transformation and enlightenment in their own way.

Take a moment now and reflect on the beings for whom you were a Star Person; who would write YOUR name in their Book of Stars with reverence and with love.

Take a moment to remember some of these moments, and what it felt like to be in the presence of someone who actually transformed right before your eyes – because you were there.

You are a Star Person.

We all are.

When we consciously understand this, and finally embrace the truth of this, we can start to think of ourselves, and of other beings, in a much more logical, constructive and loving way.

We can begin to become aware when the opportunity for transformation presents itself.

We can be consciously aware of that, and then go ahead and allow this to happen.

Helping other beings to evolve is an extraordinary experience in its own right, a Star Event that teaches us about our power to positively impact the lives of other beings.

So take a moment now and reflect on those Star Memories when you helped another evolve, and enter at least three examples of this into your Book of Stars.

Star People & The Star Matrix

Once we've become consciously aware of the Star People, all the Star Beings, and the fact that we are Star People too, the Star Matrix gains many, MANY new points of light and takes a shift into a new dimension of clarity.

The Star People help to start to connect the dots of our Star Events in a whole new way.

Having all our Star People, hard, human, or otherwise, in the same space at the same time allows us to finally understand how the transformational relationships we make actually work.

This also puts our own powers to help others evolve into a new light.

On one hand, we start to understand just how powerful we personally are, how we absolutely have the power to help others evolve. This is of course, hugely empowering! It is also a hint as to what we might want to do more of in the future, because it feels so good and it evolves us too, every time.

On the other hand, we start to understand just how many people and entities are involved in one single person's unfolding incarnation.

There are thousands of them, perhaps even more!!!

This means that YOU don't have to be the one where the buck stops, regardless of who we are dealing with. It takes a village to raise a child, and it takes a cast of thousands, and of all kinds of different entities at that, to evolve a person.

You never again have to feel solely responsible for the evolution (or healing, or education, or protection, or etc!) of another being.

All you have to do is to be "the gift that only you would have to give."

You do that, and you have discharged your responsibility to not just humanity, but to the Great Creative Order itself, in a spectacular and perfect fashion.

You are precious, and beyond prize. You are YOU. Your Star Matrix is absolutely unique in all times spent, and YOUR GIFT is to be you, at the right time, at the right moment.

It's a beautiful thing.

As our Star Matrix begins to assemble, then grow, then starts to really sparkle, our opportunities expand in turn, and then we can be consciously ready to pick up all that power and do something with it – when that moment presents itself.

Now, it's over to you.

Ask your dear Energy Mind to remind you of your first Star Person in your life, and inscribe their name in your Book of Stars.

Remember that you are searching for MOMENTS of transformation, real Star Events that changed you profoundly, and you knew you had evolved in that instance.

Add at least three more Star Beings to your Book of Stars, and continue to add more.

Your Star Beings are absolutely also "your friends in high places" and can provide you with energy and further information at any time you would need this.

Also, add at least three Star Events where you were a Star Person to another being. This is hugely empowering!

Star Powers

Every person I have ever met, without exception, has their own Star Powers –
something they are exceptionally good at, something that has always been
with them, a special skill or natural talent of some kind that has been a
golden thread throughout their current incarnation.

You can think of these Star Powers as our actual human Super Powers.

There are more than just one, but right here, right now, let's start with the first
one – your 1ˢᵗ Star Power.

The 1st Star Power

We are consciously aware of our 1st Star Power – it has manifested so many times in our lives in Star Events that we could not ignore it and had to accept the fact that we have, indeed, this one Star Power.

I am exceptionally creative. I've always been that way from a very young child onwards, and this has never wavered in all my decades on this planet. It is absolutely a Super Power that has given me innumerable Star Events along the way, got me out of all sorts of scrapes, and to this day forms the very basis of how I make my living in the Hard, as well.

What is your 1st Star Power?

If you cannot answer that question immediately, ask your dear Energy Mind:

"Dear Energy Mind! Please give me a Star Memory about my 1st Star Power."

Do the Star Matrix process properly and step by step.

Enter the Star Memory into your Book of Stars.

While you are there, and on this particular track of discovery, ask for further memories relating to your 1st Star Power.

Really understanding and connecting the events relating to your 1st Star Power is tremendously educational and empowering. This will help you get to know yourself better at a whole new level.

An important note: Star Powers like "creativity" for those who have them are instant and obvious. But Star Powers can be all sorts of things. One person discovered that their first Star Power was what they described as "patience," and I would describe as "compassion" instead. That doesn't seem so amazing but it actually is a real Super Power to remain patient/compassionate when everything around you descends into stress and chaos; and it's actually a Super Power I wish I had too.

Allow your dear Energy Mind to understand your first Super Power, and spend some time on exploring this, finding more memories relating to this, and as a result, understanding your qualities as a person much better.

More Star Powers!

Our 1st Star Power is lovely and always a tremendous source of strength, inspiration and homecoming, plus it is something that we can always develop further, take to the next level – how amazing is that going to be?

But we are not one trick ponies.

Humans have more than one Star Power.

What else is fundamental to your being?

Ask your dear Energy Mind to give you a memory of a different Star Power that has been with you, always.

You may ask for a third, a fourth, a fifth Star Power and then consider all these Star Powers side by side, how they influence each other, interact with each other, and what might happen if they really connected up and became more than the sum of their parts, or if they played out simultaneously rather than sequentially.

I also like the idea of asking myself, when I meet a person, especially one I have met many times before, "I wonder what your Star Powers are ..."

Gaining a sense of that will tell you more about that person than reading their history of trauma, illness and failure – and that is guaranteed.

Now, it's over to you.

Add at least two more Star Powers to your Book of Stars in the form of specific memories where an aspect displayed these additional Star Powers.

The more memories you add to your Book of Stars, the stronger your Star Matrix becomes, and the more interesting beneficial side effects reveal themselves, so don't sell yourself short here – take the time to do this now.

The OTHER Star Powers

We have many more fascinating skills, talents and abilities than we are consciously aware of.

There is a fascinating principle in Modern Energy and thereby, in Star Matrix, which I call 1=INFINITY.

1=INFINITY means that every event in a person's life can only happen once. No aspect is ever the same as any aspect before; no experience is ever the same as any other experience. We cannot repeat any experience; any experience stands, for all infinity.

What that means for us right here is that when you have done something once, not only does that prove that you can do this, but also, that it is done.

For example, if you have loved someone once, for that one MOMENT that defines a true Star Event, then you have loved. You can no longer say that you have never loved; it has happened, and now it's true for your life.

1=INFINITY

The same works the other way around. If some being has loved you, even just once, then you were loved.

1=INFINITY

This doesn't mean, however, that we can just stop there. Every love is different, each one is a step stone on a path that is infinite.

Each Star Event is a portal to the next one, if only we knew this.

As each Star Event is also entirely unique, and no Star Event can ever be repeated, we once more have the idea of 1=INFINITY.

What this means in the context of our OTHER Star Powers is that if you have read somebody's mind once, it proves you have the capacity for that, you can do this, and you can develop this further if you were to put your mind to it. You can use this first event as a portal to the next one.

What OTHER and further Star Powers each one of us has, and has already proven they have, is what we discover when we start looking for Star Memories of displaying amazing and/or unusual abilities.

It's our Star Memories that have the information we need to know what we can really do.

Check your memories for Star Memories relating to "The OTHER Super Powers."

This could be …

- Star Memories of exceptional strength, or speed, or physical ability;

- Star Memories of exceptional empathy, telepathy, precognition, knowing;

- Star Memories of exceptional skills, abilities, talents;

- Star Memories of expanded awareness, superconscious awareness, enlightenment experiences;

- Star Memories of paranormal abilities, psychic abilities, magic;

- Star Memories of highly unusual events that the current paradigm cannot or will not explain;

- Star Memories of exceptional mental clarity, intelligence, problem solving.

It is a most fascinating discovery that everyone has these Star Memories. Unfortunately, because our societal views of what people are and what they can do is severely limited, there is no "place" in our old constructs for this sort of thing.

Star Memories of our very real, proven, personal Super Powers in action find their place right alongside all our other Star Memories in the Star Matrix.

They are now consciously available, and we can now choose to explore these memories further, to use them as portals to more Star Events of a similar nature, to develop them further, and to encourage the emergence of other Star Powers that we are perfectly capable of.

You may have noticed the capitalisation of the word OTHER.

There is a reason for this.

People's self concepts are incredibly limited and lacking. Star Matrix is designed to change that, and to give literally a matrix where we can put our high positive memories together, so they can connect and start interact with each other, to become more than the sum of their parts.   •

People are designed to model themselves after other people; we "role model" on existing people in our environment. This has proven to be a real problem with humanity, as the roles models we have are severely lacking in brilliance and inspiration.

To get over that, I created the concept of the OTHERS.

These are human beings with fully functional energy systems, who have learned how to live life on the positive side of the Modern Energy Chart.

The OTHERS are not "superhuman" in any way, they're just human, but systemically actually finally working as they should.

The people we are when we are in the highest energy states, our Star Aspects in other words, are the OTHERS.

When we are in the high energy states, and each one of us has been in the high energy states, as proven by your Star Memories, we become the role models for humanity – and we become role models for ourselves, for our own aspects.

"Who do you want to be when you grow up?"

"I want to be my +10 self!"

Now we have a role model for ourselves, and an obvious pathway to get there.

We are entirely free of the role models of the past, and can grow into our own personal best – at any time of life.

Every single aspect of you who has experienced a Star Event became an OTHER in that moment.

And the fact is that the OTHERS do things in a different way, have access to many, many more "Super Powers" than we ever dreamed of, and are happy!

I am telling you this so you won't be too afraid to really go on a quest to find your Star Memories relating to extraordinary skills, talents and abilities.

These OTHER Star Memories are not just right and true. They are exactly the kind of thing we need to re-orientate ourselves and to find a much better, righter position for each one of us in the greater scheme of things.

They are also fascinating, as much fun as you can possibly have with your clothes on, and give us that all important trajectory we need in personal development – what we want to develop next, and most importantly, what we want to develop INTO when all is said and done.

Now, it's over to you.

Find examples of your OTHER Star Powers, and enter them in your Book of Stars.

- *I draw a little STAR behind the entries relating to Star Powers so I can spot them easily when I look through my Book of Stars.*

The Shining Stars

By now, you should have quite a few entries in your Book of Stars.

You should also be able to freely discover more positive memories simply by asking your dear Energy Mind.

In other words, you have started to build a new network of pathways in your physical brain through which information can flow, and new pathways in your energy body, through which new energy can flow.

We've achieved this by directing our attention on the Star Memories, the Star Aspects, and the Star Moments of our lives, and it's becoming ever easier to make this movement in the right direction, to where the Star Memories are stored.

Now it's time to put this newfound skill to good use, and have us aid us in reality creation in a whole new way.

This is very powerful, and I would say, this alone will change your life, especially as time goes by.

So, what are The Shining Stars?

Let's start with the opposite, because this is of course, super familiar to us all.

There is a joke which goes as follows.

> *"What is the worst form of Alzheimers?"*
>
> *"When you only remember the insults!"*

In a nutshell, this is what our trauma fixation has created for us all.

People literally only remember the insults.

Be that …

- Family members who only remember that dreadful thing with the potato salad at Aunt Betty's 60th birthday party, twenty years ago, and nobody has spoken to anybody since (!);

- A wonderful artist who only remembers that one horrendous customer who said they hated their art and demanded their money back, and which caused them to never put another picture up for sale, not for the last 15 years;

- A person who had once been betrayed by just one friend, and now has no friends, wants no friends, and has been grumpy, bitter and angry ever since;

- The youngster who got 31 excellent birthday and Xmas presents from their parents, but only remembers the ONE time where they forgot;

- The other youngster who was picked up from school and endless other activities a thousand times, but only remembers the ONE time when the parents didn't turn up on time;

- The business owner who has thousands of excellent customers, but they only remember the one rotten apple who caused so much trouble ...

"Remembering only the insults" is EVERYWHERE, everybody's doing it, and it literally creates more of the same horrible, negative reality simply by focus of attention, and the following lowering of energy into the negative states, where a person becomes stupid, limited, unattractive and forsaken by luck, love or happiness.

- **I cannot overstate just how powerfully reality creating the choice of focusing on the negative VS focusing on the positive actually is.**

The example of the business owner is the easiest to follow.

The business owner is completely in charge of their business.

They write the advertisements, set the tone, "talk to" someone out there, and who is that they are talking to?

A business owner who has been burned by a bad customer, dropped down the energy chart, and is now "thinking about the bad customer" in the back of their mind when they do anything relating to their business will obviously attract more of the same – whilst, at the same time, losing rapport with the GOOD customers, and never mind the EXCELLENT, STAR CUSTOMERS which they should be thinking about and addressing instead.

Now this is a master metaphor.

Have a think how that exact pattern plays out with a person who has been burned by a bad dating partner, and now, and with that in mind, creates their new dating profile. Who are they talking to, and who will they attract? Will they be attracting a STAR DATE?

Can you understand how this works?

Can you understand what a simply enormous difference it would make to the practical results these people were going to get if they switched their focus consciously from the bad apples to the STAR PEOPLE in their context?

Try this for yourself now.

Think of a bad apple type person who has hurt you, traumatized you, done you harm, and you think of them often and reflexively. This can be in any context you choose, friends, teachers, partners, family members, customers, clients, co-workers.

As you have thought of them so often and so reflexively, we have the established train tracks ready to go and they pop up right away.

Notice how your happy energy state is going down as soon as you connect with that negative memory.

We're only going to do this once, so that you can really feel and sense how this affects you, instantly.

Now, on the same topic, we're going to focus on a Shining Star instead – a Star Moment with a wonderful person that was powerfully positive and highly transformative, inspirational for you.

Don't skip this. Give it a go.

Assume the Heart Position.

Breathe deeply.

Think Star Matrix, think in the opposite direction.

- **Remember a Shining Star.**

Now pay attention to this totally different person, and how, when you connect with that energy instead, you immediately become uplifted, energized and inspired.

Now physically point in the direction of this Shining Star example and say out aloud, "I want many, many more Shining Stars in my life!"

Then give yourself and your Shining Star a heartfelt round of applause.

Do it now and reap the rewards!

This base pattern is the key to "winning friends and influencing people."

This base pattern is the key to setting a brand new direction towards more and more wonderful Star People and Star Experiences with Shining Stars in your own life.

For almost every form of human interaction, there is a Shining Star example that you can draw on, literally, to empower you in the right way, in the right context, and to power your ship of life in the right direction for a change.

From this much better energy state, you act differently, and your actions have different results.

It's a beautiful thing, and if you learn only one thing from this entire book, enacting the Shining Star pattern in your life from this moment forth will bring you a better future.

Shining Star Aspects

Now in this original Shining Star pattern above, we are talking about different individuals to focus on – the "bad apple" is one person, and the "Shining Star" is another person.

We can apply this pattern to a single person and their aspects if we choose to do so.

In a very long term relationship, as is found in families and life time partnerships, we will be dealing with one person who has been both a Shining Star at one time, and a bad apple at another.

Here, we can also choose to focus on the Shining Star aspects, and please note, we can CHOOSE to do that if we want to.

Energetically speaking, it's the right thing to do, and it may well encourage the occurrence of more and better aspects in that one person over time.

In child rearing, this is of course of the essence.

However, it is entirely up to you how you choose to apply this principle in your life.

Focusing on the Shining Stars is always the right thing to do; that's where the true wisdom lies, the most information, and the highest examples of what a person can be.

Other people's Shining Star aspects, just like our own Shining Star aspects, our Star Aspects, are the key to evolution, on the individual level, on the level of the family, on the level of society and on the level of humanity itself.

Now, it's over to you.

Enter Shining Star memories in your Book of Stars now.

Particularly find Shining Star memories in the contexts that have given you personally the most problems in your life.

Pay attention to things in your past that you stopped doing or gave up on altogether because of the bad apple and find Shining Stars to end that obsession of failure.

By doing this, you will gain the ability to recognise when "only remembering the insults" pops up in your daily life, when you're remembering the one bad apple among an entire truckload of wonderful ones.

Train your attention to find the very best, highest Shining Stars to inspire you, uplift you, and give you whole new ideas on how to deal with very real challenges in your life.

This is how we create a different reality.

Star Light

A particularly fascinating class of Star Memories are about funny memories – Star Light memories.

When we rise up on the Modern Energy Chart, we become literally lighter, more light-filled, less dour, less heavy, more shiny, more sparkly.

Spontaneous outbursts of laughter are the fastest way to be catapulted up the Energy Chart; it feels like fireworks are exploding in our energy bodies and changing our state in a heartbeat.

Likewise, accessing Star Memories of laughter raises our energy states fast and helps us regain perspective and personal power in an instance.

When we speak with others, exchanging Star Light memories brings life and energy into the deepest and darkest group gatherings and that includes funerals, and soldiers under fire.

I consider Star Light experiences to be right up there with our best enlightenment experiences, and my own memories of bursting out in explosive laughter are some of my most valuable "Treasures & Riches."

The easiest way to get into Star Light memories with yourself or others is to ask about a favourite comedian who has made you laugh so much, you nearly cried. This comedian is also a Star Person whose name belongs in your Book of Stars!

Once you start asking for Star Light memories, many, many more examples will come to you.

Like many other forms of Star Memories, Star Light memories seem to be grouped together and far away from the enlightenment experiences that felt hugely spiritual at the time; but when we connect them up with all our other Star Memories, they bring that essential sparkle and JOY, laughter, back into the entire Star Matrix, making it sparkle and making it much, much lighter.

We found that talking to other family members about moments of spontaneous laughter, remembering funny events together is extraordinary in its effect on how much energy, love and connection flows between them.

Giving attention to your own Star Aspects, visiting with your own personal most profound Star Light experiences, will not only raise your energy significantly and instantly; it will also "teach" you a lot about the energy system, and how quickly it can explode into joy when it is triggered to do so.

I would also invite you to consider times when your aspects made other people laugh. That's an amazing Super Power in its own right; and to find out more about how that works is hugely evolutionary and literally, priceless.

Now it's over to you!

Ask your dear Energy Mind to send you a Star Light memory of your own – something that made you laugh out aloud, something really, really funny.

Note how your energy state changes when you even think about this.

Then tell the Star Light story out aloud, really allow yourself to get into it, and also pay attention what was learned, understood or resolved through this particular Star Event.

Be sure to pay attention to humour and laughter in the future. This is a hugely overlooked and under-explored mystery of the human energy system that really is amazing in the effects it has on Mind, Body and Spirit all at the same time.

And when you are with someone else, and the energy is miserable, keep it in the back of your mind to say, "Tell me a funny story!"

Intermission

There is a good chance that you are "binge reading" this entire book and you haven't actually stopped to do the exercises when I wrote, "**And now, it's over to you ...**"

This is the difference between reading a book, and taking a course, in a nutshell.

In a course, live or distance learning, you are "forced" to do the all the exercises properly, one after the other, in the right order and sequence, and so you learn the new things in the right order and sequence, one exercise building on the next, until we're left, in this case, with the Star Matrix as the inevitable result.

What happens next here, in this book, is that I'm going to tell you about the reason for doing all of this – the Star Matrix, or more precisely, YOUR Star Matrix, is the goal, the outcome, the gain, the prize of the processes.

What I would like you to understand is that by simply reading this book, you will have lots of new ideas and insights, and that's a marvellous start.

The real prize here, discovering and KNOWING your own Star Matrix, can only happen when you have done the "work," and this includes that you have:

- Actively attempted to remember high positive memories, the Star Events;
- Become consciously aware of these Star Memories;
- Spoken your Star Memories out aloud and made them real in your living energy body, here and now;
- Spent at least a little time on connecting with the aspects who had these Star Events;
- Spent at least a little time reflecting on the messages, meanings, and inherent WISDOM in these Star Events;
- Had the time to ask other people about their Star Events, because that gives us the much bigger picture on Star Events and how they work in general;

... and most of all, have entered at least 20 but preferably many more of your own Star Events into your Book of Stars.

Every Star Memory recovered is an important puzzle piece in its own right.

- **We can't tell what the "big picture" is when we don't have enough pieces yet.**

We can't conceptualise the Star Matrix correctly, and the dots can't connect when there aren't enough of them.

I hope this makes sense to you, and encourages you to go on and start remembering more and more Star Events, Star People, Star Moments and Star Experiences that will go into your Book of Stars.

The more information you have, the more Star Memories you have consciously become aware of, the easier and clearer the entire Star Matrix becomes.

The second part of this book is now about the Star Matrix itself; the methods and meditations here become obvious, natural and self perpetuating when you have collected enough Star Memories.

If you cannot make the Star Matrix itself work for you or it is nebulous, a little too far away, too theoretical, not entirely manifest to the degree that you can absolutely feel the shift in your own living body, here and now, then simply continue to add to your Star Memory collection.

Put it in your diary and add one Star Memory a day to your Book of Stars.

More and more will come to you; and that is even before we start with the Missing Events.

We need to know what's already there so we can then know what is missing, or needs to done.

That's the key to Star Matrix.

Star Lives

Missing Events

The moment you start talking about the Missing Events, people's ears prick up.

Of course! With so much trauma and so little love, our Star Matrix must be like a giant sieve, full of holes, in fact, it must be more like a black hole that greedily sucks in all the tiny bits of love that randomly come its way …

We must have a billion missing events, and that's why our lives aren't working as they should!

I am laughing to myself writing this, because I used to believe that too.

It's a side effect of only focusing on the negative and totally "forgetting" about all the good things that have happened in our lives.

Please let me be clear here.

1. Yes, absolutely, there is a good chance we are missing key events that would have helped us create a much more stable and powerful events matrix. Human societal organisation and child rearing is so profoundly weird, it would be most surprising if that wasn't the case.

   BUT! And that's a big BUT in capslock …

2. **We have nowhere near as many missing events as we think we do; and**

3. **Before we go creating missing events, we must ALWAYS check if a Star Event on the topic already exists.**

   This is truly, super fascinating and will tell you more about "who you really are" than just about anything else from the Star Matrix universe.

To check for missing events and finding that they have indeed already occurred, and probably more than once as well, gives us a wonderful opportunity to correct deeply flawed self concepts and misunderstandings about ourselves in an easy, elegant and incontrovertible way.

This is also a huge step forward in personal development on every level.

For example, a person might cry, "I have never known true love!" They might even burst out into tears and, if left unchecked, are on the road to their own personal dark night of the soul experience … yet again …

Before we go ahead and create a missing event of "knowing true love" we want to check our existing inventory of Star Events.

We ask the person to assume the Heart Position and think of something they love, to raise their energy. When they are ready, we ask them to ask their dear Energy Mind for a true love memory.

What happens next …?

The curious and wonderful thing is that 9 times out of 10, a Star Memory comes to mind, and often, it is profoundly surprising to our person.

One person remembered holding a newborn kitten and loving it so endlessly, it changed their world in a Star Moment of pure love. This person cried out in astonishment, "I thought love was about receiving love, not … giving it … feeling it … BEING IT …"

We might ask them, "Do you now need to construct a missing event about knowing true love?" and this person shook their head most congruently and said, "Oh no, I know true love alright!"

So if that's not the missing event we want to create, what other missing event could we be searching for?

The person thought about it and said eventually, "I guess what I'm missing is … being the newborn kitten, receiving that kind of … love? Adoration? Oh, it's so beyond words …"

That sound reasonable, but let's check first. Dear Energy Mind, do I have a Star Memory of being loved beyond words ..?

Again, the person was totally surprised to immediately receive a memory of having a moment with a pet dog, looking into the animal's eyes and receiving that sense of being more than the whole world to this creature, being everything there could ever be.

The person said, "I have loved, and I was loved. I know love! Oh my …"

Yes. Oh my …

Wisdom is in the Star Moments. We learn here what matters, and how things work.

Now this person doesn't have to wander the Earth looking for something that was found already, a long time ago, and many times in different guises, in different flavours, each experience adding to their knowing of how to give love and how to receive it too.

Now this person can start to wonder what missing events they might really need, and that is simply a question our Conscious Minds cannot answer.

We consciously do not know enough about the workings of ourselves as multidimensional beings in a multidimensional multiverse!

Luckily for us, our partner in life, our dear Energy Mind, knows more about what our person is, as well as what they need, than we consciously do.

So we are going to leave the creation of missing events to our dear Energy Minds, enter into the process happily, and learn some truly new and surprising facts about ourselves along the way.

To re-iterate: What we THINK are our major missing events is virtually guaranteed to be incorrect.

In fact, the act of first of all asking our dear Energy Minds for the events we thought we didn't have, and receiving those, will stand us in much better stead when it comes to creating missing events.

False Memories & The Energy System

In the 1980s, it became popular in Psychology to try and retrieve trauma memories that a person did not remember through a combination of hypnosis, drugs and suggestion. This caused a huge spike in court cases and criminal prosecutions brought against the perpetrators, many of whom absolutely refused to acknowledge that such events had ever taken place.

The term "false memory syndrome" was coined, and many experiments were conducted on how easy it may be to create false memories in adults and children.

It turned out that it was very easy and did not require either hypnosis or drugs.

A researcher was sent into a school class of ordinary children from many different cultural backgrounds, once a week for 8 weeks, and he invited the children to tell him about their class hamster.

He simply said, "Tell me about the class hamster!"

The first week, the children agreed that they never had a class hamster.

On his second visit, some children responded by saying that they had had a class hamster, but it had died.

By his final visit on week 8, there was no child left who disagreed with the fact that there had been indeed, a class hamster, and that it had died. The children could also now tell stories of what it had been like to stroke the class hamster, details of its character, the name, the colour of the cage and much besides.

Importantly, many of the children showed strong emotional responses, crying and becoming emotionally distraught, when remembering and talking about the death of the class hamster.

We can learn the following from this.

1. The Energy Mind is a CREATOR of memories. A generator which can create anything at all and this can become a memory.

2. This memory affects the energy body exactly as all other memories will.

3. The effect on the energy body produces emotions, emotional states and our energy body states, which are depicted on the Modern Energy Chart.

4. We ask the questions and the Energy Mind answers.

5. **We can create energy body states and emotions by using that system.**

Of course, the myopic focus on trauma took all this research into the wrong direction by 180' and caused more chaos, disturbance and insanity, when the possibility for a glorious application existed at the same time that was never probably investigated.

Here is another example of misuse of the extraordinary generator of experiences that is our dear Energy Mind.

Past Life Regression

The great hobby of the New Agers at the same time as False Memory Syndrome appeared in Psychology was Past Life Regression.

The idea went as follows.

If you have problems now, and you can't find any trauma to explain this in this life, and you can't find any birth trauma or pre-birth trauma, then the trauma must have occurred in a Past Life.

By going back to re-visit the past life trauma, the past life trauma is cleared and produces beneficial results in this life.

This is the old trauma story all over again, but the problem with trauma is that if we ask the Energy Mind for trauma, it will give us trauma – literally endlessly, infinitely, because it is a GENERATOR rather than a bucket that can be emptied.

I also noted this in the days of tapping on energy points, using negative set ups. The dear, dear Energy Mind will generate infinite answers to the question, "What is wrong with me?" or "Where's the next trauma?" which will likewise lead to tapping forever.

The structure of "creating trauma → visiting trauma → releasing trauma" is unfortunately not a game with a positive outcome for the energy body.

It is exhausting, harrowing, and the more often this game is played, the more the energy system depletes, and the more chaotic it becomes over time.

- **The trauma game is a negative sum game which leads to more chaos and insanity, not to more empowerment or better mental health.**

The exact same system directed in the opposite direction, used to generate likewise infinite Star Memories in order to learn from them, has likewise the exact opposite effect on the energy system.

Creating Star Memories not only delights us, enriches us and empowers us.

Using this system wisely has the potential to give us a whole new level of control over our own incarnations.

The Star Lives

There are many ways to create missing events for our Star Matrix; I decided to focus on the Star Lives as this is a direct, simple and easy way to create brand new Star Memories for ourselves, but without getting them mixed up with our existing memories.

Let us consider that our own Star Memories exist forever at the energy levels, and they can exist there because they are energy rich, strong, and cohesive.

Other people's Star Events also exist there, and this space is non-temporal, non-linear.

This means we don't have to search for "past" lives but we can have access to ANY Star Event, from any person (or entity), past, present, future and anywhere else.

The Star Life Pattern is a simple set of questions that the Conscious Mind asks, and the dear Energy Mind will answer, by creating the perfect Star Life with its perfect Star Memory for us.

This is what the dear Energy Minds do; it is natural, easy, and super-interesting, super-enlightening.

Moreover, you can do this as many times as you want, and there is a POSITIVE pay off for your energy system at the end that keeps accumulating.

We might say that the endless quest for trauma will drive us insane, and the endless quest for Star Memories will drive us sane! :-)

In the Star Life Pattern, we ask the Energy Mind to create a complete person (a persona) for us who has experienced the exact Star Events we are missing.

First, we let the Energy Mind create the persona, and then take us to the pivotal event in that Star Person's life. This is our missing event.

We can then experience this event from different perspectives and also inhabit the person at the moment of their Star Event so we experience the energy movements we need for our own Star Matrix.

Here is the Star Life Pattern for you to experience.

The Star Life Pattern

1. Start with the Three Levels Meditation; this is important so we are communicating clearly that we are interested in getting information and experiences from the highest level, where the Stars are.

2. Assume the Heart Position and make the Set Up. "Dear Energy Mind! Connect me with the perfect Star Life for me today!" (You can leave it up to the Energy Mind to choose, which is what I prefer, or put a direction in the Set Up, "... connect me with the perfect Star Life that can help me with my problem X today!")

3. Now ask the following set of questions out aloud, and answer them out aloud.

   ○ Is this Star Person male, female or other?

   ○ What is their hair colour? Eye colour? Skin colour?

   ○ What are they wearing?

   ○ What else is important about them?

   ○ What is their job, occupation or mission?

   ○ Do they have a family? Friends?

   ○ Where do they come from?

   ○ Take a moment to familiarise yourself with this person and their world, their life.

4. Now assume the Heart Position and ask your dear Energy Mind to take you to that special Star Moment in this person's life we are here to share. Use the Classic Game SuperMind questions if the information comes too fast to keep consciously track of.

   The Star Event in this person's life we're here to share:

   ○ What was the time of day when it happened?

   ○ What was the time of year?

   ○ What was the weather or atmosphere?

   ○ What was the landscape or surroundings?

- ○ What else was there?
- ○ What happened next?

5. When you have that Star Event, take some time to discover the energy, the sensations, the information and most importantly, the CONNECTION – why this one Star Event was so important for you to have in your own Star Matrix now, what it means for the past, the present and the future.

6. Add the Star Event and your Star Life Persona to your Book of Stars to make it official.

Trusting Your Dear Energy Mind

Our dear Energy Mind knows more about our energy systems across the levels and layers than we can ever consciously know.

I know we're all consciously hung up on various ideas of what missing events we really need, but seriously, we know very little!

I would invite you to trust your dear Energy Mind to create your missing Star Events for you without prejudice, allow yourself to be surprised by what you get, and what else you'll get if you ask for the next and the next Star Life event.

This is endlessly fascinating, and with a positive Set Up towards moments of love and enlightenment, we just can't go wrong.

We have such beautiful, amazing minds when they work together as they were originally designed to work.

The Conscious Mind and the Energy Mind in harmony are The SuperMind.

The Future Stars

I invited someone to join the Star Matrix course, and they said, "Bah, it's only about old memories, not interested, thanks."

I was absolutely astonished for a moment and realised that in the sheer joy of discovering all these beautiful memories, each one a shining jewel, so precious, so beloved and so amazing, I had forgotten to include the whole reason for Star Matrix in the advertising!

- **The whole reason for Star Matrix are the FUTURE STARS!**

The past has been and gone, and continues to slide away behind us; we're here and now, where we are always acting, and before us lies the future.

Star Matrix is about learning how to have a much, much, MUCH brighter future!

Of course it is!

I have the funny feeling that by all that attention to trauma and digging for trauma, and even creating new trauma (as in the Past Life Regression of old!) we have been giving all the wrong signals to ourselves, each other, and potentially our invisible friends at all levels!

With our actions and intentions, surely it must seem to everyone that we want more trauma in our lives!

It is a veritable miracle that we are not going from one catastrophe to the next … oh, wait a minute … hmmm …

So let me be clear!

- **Star Matrix is about learning what Star Memories are, how they happen, what they do to us, and most of all, about learning how to have more of them!**

As many Star Memories as possible before we shuffle off our mortal coils and our soul starts soaring in joy!

Let us start right here, with the absolute declaration, "YES! I want more Star Events in my life!"

Saying YES! To Star Events

In The Power of the Positives, we have the YES! Scale.

It's basically the Modern Energy Chart – on the negative side, you have NO, and on the positive side, you have YES.

What we see when we do that is right away that there are different degrees of YES!

- A +3 yes is a little yes, with only 30% of power of YES.

- A +5 yes has 50% chance of success, of reality creating.

- **A +10 YES!!! is a big yes, a full power 100% YES!!!**

We want to say a +10 YES!!! to having more Star Events in our lives, because a +10 YES!!! rings the Universe like a bell, and changes will then happen.

Don't be afraid of changing the status quo to which you may have clung for a long time.

Don't be afraid of a truly starry future – a fun future, an easy, effortless and exciting future, full of surprises, full of amazing experiences, full of AHA! Moments, delighted laughter, and dancing with sheer joy.

If you are scared, worried or reversed about creating real CHANGE in your life, and therefore, in the lives of others around you, I can tell you – it's only energy!

More energy means more love, and that's not only the right direction to be moving towards, it is the ONLY choice if we want to live up to our own potential.

Let's say YES!!! to our starry futures!

Let's take a deep breath, assume the Heart Position, and make that statement:

"I want more Star Events in my life! I say YES!!! to Star Events!"

I would like you to do this in your own time, using any energy method you know, until your YES!!! to Star Events is a +10 YES!!! - totally empowered, not a shred of doubt remaining, an absolute declaration of intention that is heard by all of you, on all levels and layers, and everyone else who is assisting you on every level in this incarnation and beyond.

Saying your own personal +10 YES!!! to the Star Events is a Star Event in its own right.

It is the moment future aspects will look back upon, loving it, deriving inspiration from it, the moment your life changed for the better.

So here we are, creating our first real Star Event deliberately, for a purpose, with intention; a precious treasure for all our aspects and as I suspect, a long missing event.

Who do you want to be when you grow up? This was a question I could never answer before, but now I know exactly who I want to be.

I want to be a collector of Star Events!

I say YES!!! to Star Events!

The Star Line

As long as we are still breathing, we are virtually guaranteed to have more Star Events in our lives. People are designed to have these events which evolve their energy systems, make them richer, more sparkly and more powerful with each and every Star Memory collected.

When we consciously say YES!!! to the Star Events, and direct our attention to the ones we've already experienced, thus learning how "Star Events happen" at a structural level, we gain access to many more Star Events in the future.

I would like you now to simply consider your future, a pathway stretching out in front of you, and it is sparkling with the Future Stars still to come.

I would like you to note that there is no end to this Star Line – it continues on, unbroken by physical death, into the post-physical existence where the soul itself continues to have Star Events of its own, because that's how thing evolve at the energy levels.

Take a moment to be here with your very own Star Line, and allow yourself to experience a sense of true wonder at the beauty of this, the sheer love inherent in this.

Also notice that this, your very own Star Line, forms a path.

It has a direction, it has a trajectory.

We could call it our destiny, if we wanted to.

If we were to rise higher, so that we could conceive more of this Star Line, we would see that our past is on this path as well.

Our Star Events are not random, they are not isolated.

They are the way markers on a much bigger story, a truthful story about your existence, and all the things you've learned that are important about life.

The Star Line is a thing of beauty.

Everyone has their own Star Line.

It's the most wonderful thing to consciously connect with, to spend time with, to explore.

We might want to ask our dear Energy Mind to take us to a future star, and gain a sense of what a future aspect who is having a Star Moment is experiencing.

We can connect with this future aspect using the SuperMind Classic Game, and we can learn things that are important for us to have learned, right here and now.

We can use the Star Line to connect with past aspects as well, and if we ever lose our sense of destiny, our own Star Line is the place to go to remember our path and purpose, our mission, our unique and personal true journey towards the light.

We can use this information to make course corrections in our current incarnations, to relieve stress and tensions, letting go of what is not important, and becoming focused on the things that really matter for each and every one of us.

The Star Line sparkles away the fear of the future, and connecting with our own Star Line often and with the excitement of learning more about it, discovering more about it, creates a steady and resonant connection that may well become a lifeline in moments of crisis.

The Star Stories – Stories Of Enlightenment

We have been falsely taught that lists of "facts" contain more information than a "story." We have been literally brainwashed to doubt eye witness testimonials as "unreliable," and the greatest insult of all is the absolute dismissal of "anecdotal evidence" in our current soulless so called science.

Now hear this.

- **Our personal stories are the only truth about life for a human being.**

Our memories and our life experiences are the only facts that matter – to each one of us, and to all of us collectively.

There are always those who will feed us lies upon lies to control us, manipulate us, milk us for our time, energy, efforts for their own nefarious purposes.

Our memories are the truth; and when we put them together, we start to understand the greater truth about what it means to be a human being in this universe of ours, at this time.

Instead of endlessly being "blinded by science" (and I mean that literally!), we need to start to talk to each other once more, exchange information, **learn from each other.**

We do that through our Star Stories.

Every Star Story is literally, a "story of enlightenment."

The aspects had an enlightenment experience; that's what made it a Star Event.

They either learned something brand new, something they never knew before; or they experienced the expansion of something already familiar into a whole new level of wonder and magnitude.

I cannot overestimate what the telling of our own Star Stories does for our minds, our bodies and our spirits. I literally can not.

Yet, that's only the beginning.

When another person receives a Star Story from someone else, they are receiving "an education in Star Events" - always.

An expansion of their own ideas of what Star Events are; a reminder of their own Star Events; a lighting of hope that they too can have further such Star Events of their own; they receive energy, information, love and assistance on their paths, whether they realise it, or not.

Your Star Stories are absolutely the gifts that only you would have to give.

Your Star Stories are unique, priceless – they are Treasures & Riches, sparkling jewels of the greatest value and worth, and they don't diminish when we freely share them with each other.

Humanity needs to start consciously collecting their Star Stories afresh; focusing on these; we need to put all of our Star Stories together, and when we do, we understand who we human beings really are.

Sharing Your Star Stories

I think of every single Star Story as a ball of light – a Star, in other words. The human world is so stressed and so energy poor, every ball of light is going to help!

Star Stories shared directly, human to human, are the easiest and most natural way to give those gifts that only you would have to give, but there are many other ways to share your Stars.

We can write our Star Stories down and share them in that way. I like this because many more people get to have at least a connection and awareness of the energy and information of the Star Story.

We can use our Stars, our balls of light, as the inspiration for fiction stories.

We can use poetry to perhaps even better explain or express the experience in words that go beyond linear language.

We can paint pictures that capture the Star Moments and transmit the energy that way.

We can create songs and dances to transmit the energy.

Our own Star Stories provide literally endless inspiration and they want to be shared!

In this context, also watch out for all the different times and places where exactly this has already happened – where a person has created something amazing, based on what they learned during a Star Event.

A famous cook may speak of that one time where they were a child and had a Star Event in a restaurant; an architect may tell of a time when they saw something in nature and they've been designing their buildings based on this ever since.

I personally realised during my own first explorations into Star Matrix that every single "therapy pattern" or "personal development technique" I have ever created comes directly from my own Star Events with clients, friends, family, strangers, animals, nature – and what's amazing about that is that I had no idea that was how it worked. I would have a Star Experience, learned something new, and encoded this into a pattern that other people can run, and experience a similar outcome.

I have also been truly astonished to learn that my works of art likewise, are always based on a Star Experience – it's a most wonderful thing to find out that we have these Treasures & Riches we have already used unconsciously to shape our lives!

Now, and knowing that this is so, we can take our personal "creativity" to a whole new level.

You need inspiration for ... (spicing up your relationship, creating a marketing campaign, making a sparkling and positive work of art, lifting up a conversation anytime, anywhere; brightening your day, or your night; when you need a good idea for anything at all)?

You will find the PERFECT INSPIRATION in your very own Aladdin's cave of overflowing Treasures & Riches – in your very own Star Memories!

Bringing The Star Stories Back

In order to get many, many more people to break free from the endlessly destructive trauma labyrinth, I am calling upon YOU to help us all bring the Star Stories back.

Bring them back in word, song, dance, voice, art, science – everywhere.

Put out your Star Stories anyway that feels right to you, in any format you choose.

Do this deliberately, and do this right away.

The world of humans is in desperate need of high positive energy input, everywhere and on every level, from the purely personal one-on-one all the way to humanity itself across time.

Every person matters here. This isn't something we can leave to some authority to start decreeing that instead of misery, we'll be doing love, light, energy, intelligence and information all of a sudden.

Every single person who starts sharing their Star Stories adds to the sparkle of humanity itself.

This means YOU, specifically.

Find a way to tell your Star Stories.

Look for new ways in which you can share your Star Stories.

PLEASE encourage and support others who are sharing their Star Stories, because as it stands right now, they will most likely be met with "What is this? I thought we only want to ever talk about trauma and our problems and complain about them?"

Stand firm in love when it comes to "the battle of the Positives," which obviously includes positive memories, where people will tell you that working with positive energy is somehow wrong, or bad for you or anyone else.

But most importantly of all, find a way to share the Star Moments of your life.

They are precious beyond prize – not just to you, for us all.

Harvesting From The Tree Of Lights

"Harvesting From The Tree Of Lights" is my personal metaphor for using our Star Memories for personal gain across the levels and layers, and including the Hard.

Your Book of Stars is a fascinating ledger, an unfolding inventory of your Treasures & Riches; we could also say, it is a collection of energy and information.

It is more than that.

Your Book of Stars holds the data points of a multi-dimensional sculpture that is your Star Matrix – so far.

It is a model that is still incomplete.

Once you have 30, 50 or 100 Star Memory data points, you can clearly perceive where there are entire sections that are still waiting to be activated.

There are gaps, but only in our consciously accessible information, our Star Matrix map, because the structure tells us that the information must be there, or this whole thing could not work at all.

If you have a good number of Star Memories and Star People in your Book of Stars, you can begin to notice where those gaps are. For example, in my Book of Stars were no entries at all between age 8 and 11, or 1967 and 1970 respectively.

I discovered this one afternoon by looking through my own Book of Stars and found it fascinating.

By then, however, I was well practised in both asking for Star Memories, and receiving them; and the moment I asked the question, "What on Earth had happened there???" my dear Energy Mind flashed me up a Star Memory that explained it all.

The "missing three years" were immediately after the transfer from the little school for little kids to the chaotic enormous school for big kids and teenagers.

The Star Memory my dear Energy Mind had sent me was of skating on a frozen river that ran behind the school in an absolutely fantastic sparkling winter wonderland, away from the school, and the young child had a joyful shamanic out of body experience on that day.

Indeed, that was such an amazing Star Event that in 2001, a much older aspect, 34 years later (!), immortalised it in the HypnoDream "Ice River," from Wisdom of the Water, without having any idea whatsoever "where that had come from" at the time.

That one Star Memory unlocked an entire cascade of other Star Memories relating to that time in the aspect's life, that school, and beyond, and the Star Matrix took a shift that was wonderfully noticeable, and made connections across the board for me.

Without the "data points" marked out clearly on the pages in the Book of Stars, I would never have "gone looking" for memories from that time, and to not have those connections would have been a personal tragedy for me.

Writing this today has once again had the effect that I sense my aspects shaking hands across time and space, connecting with each other: the 8 year old child who skated the river; the 42 year old writer of the HypnoDreams; and the 60 year old writer of "Star Matrix," right here, right now.

It's a wonderful experience that I wish with all my heart for you; there is nothing quite like it, and from an energy perspective, it feels immensely healing as well as being strangely encouraging for the future.

"Aspects shaking hands across time and space" and smiling at each other, (re)connecting what felt like a broken timeline with so many twists and turns into a smooth and flowing river of liquid light is one those ways in which we can gather in our harvest, how we get to now finally start harvesting from our own trees of light.

I find it endlessly fascinating just how great a relief it is to finally understand something consciously that was always there, but we just couldn't connect the dots.

Now, we can.

We can use our Book of Stars to identify the missing areas and directly go there, to light up whole new sections of our Star Matrix, make it stronger, wider, wiser and more resonant.

We can also look at the themes and messages from our Star Events.

When we have enough Star Memories to compare, we want to always ask the question, "What is the same?" (and not, "What is different?" which takes you away from the bigger picture into a chaos of confusing micro components and details that do nothing to tell us anything about the real structure!).

"What is the same?" is the question that takes us to the deep structure, and the deep structure in Star Matrix is something we might as well call "your destiny."

When you have enough data points, enough Star Memories, it becomes incontrovertible that there is a theme here, that there is a structure to your existence.

Our lives are not random.

Our actions across our lives, chaotic and incident driven as they may appear, are not chaotic at all.

We are – all of us! - trying to live our destinies.

Once we get a personal sense of what that actually is, what that means, there is a sensation as though all the Star Aspects start to align behind you, empower you, have your back and help empower you into the future in a whole new way.

This is supremely metaphysical as well as being perfectly logical at the same time, and our dear Conscious Minds can understand it too.

We don't have to blindly trust that something good will happen.

We can engage in a whole new way when we start to get a sense of what each one of us is all about, and have our proof positive that there really is such a thing as your own personal destiny – your Star Memories of this lifetime.

The Star Matrix

Here we come to the final part of the Star Matrix journey – and this is the Star Matrix itself.

Only today I saw a post on social media which read:

> *My scars do not define me.*
>
> *They ARE me.*
>
> *Reminders of what is ...*

My question is, do you want a Scar Matrix – which is exactly what that is when someone says that "their scars ARE me"!!! - or do you want a **STAR MATRIX**?

Who do you want to be when you grow up?

What is so extraordinary is the fact that we can choose one or the other.

You can choose a self concept made of your scars, and live in your scar matrix; or you can choose a self concept made from the Stars, and live in your Star Matrix instead.

It's a simple choice, a conscious choice.

We don't need to tap on this first; we don't need to go to a retreat and sit in a sweat tent for ten days.

Who do you want to be when you grow up?

Someone who defines themselves by their scars, or by their Stars?

Do you want to choose to be weak, or strong; a victim or a hero?

This choice was never offered to any of us before.

Trapped in the "Nightmare of Trauma," along with everyone else, we didn't even know we had this choice.

The complete positive side of the Modern Energy Scale was and is conceptually absent in the Hard at this time; and it's beyond high time for a (r)Evolution. I wrote a book of this title a little while back and finally coming out of the Star Matrix closet is a part of this (r)Evolution.

I now offer this alternative choice to living in the scar matrix.

It is delightful, simple, so, so natural and makes perfect sense in the context of people's real behaviours and the structure of human intelligence, memory and experience.

- **Your Star Matrix is absolutely real, and it is incredibly powerful.**

With every high positive memory recovered, the Star Matrix becomes stronger.

Instead of isolated moments of bliss and enlightenment we begin to notice CONNECTIONS between these Star Events.

It is in these connections that your Star Matrix begins to take shape, become more clearly defined, begins to show you the structure of an entity that is you.

The Star Matrix is a natural, self perpetuating process that begins once we start to remember the Star Events of our own lived lives.

You don't have to work at it any further than simply adding more and more Star Events to your Book of Stars. The more you add, the more clearly the Star Matrix becomes defined, and the more powerful it will affect your energy system, and therefore, your entire life, on all levels and in all ways.

This process is as beautiful and as mysterious as watching a huge tree grow from a tiny seed.

Here is the Star Matrix Modern Energy Meditation that helps the dear Conscious Mind understand.

The Star Matrix Modern Energy Meditation

This is a version of the Three Levels Meditation.

Find yourself before a mirror. Assume the Heart Position and look into your own eyes.

1. Become aware of the pure physical being reflected there. Close your eyes and take a deep breath in and out.

2. Open your eyes afresh. Become aware of the judgements of the Hard imposed upon this being. Also notice any hard interference on the physical being, such as hair styles, adornments etc. Keep breathing deeply in the Heart Position. Close your eyes and take a deep breath in and out.

3. Open your eyes and become aware of the level of the Stars, the Star Matrix of this being. Take all the time you need to connect with your Star Matrix. When you feel complete, bow your head to the Star Being and leave.

I would encourage you to do this version of the Three Levels Meditation often, and to activate it consciously every time you not only look into a mirror, but catch your reflection anywhere you pass.

A Brand New Self Concept

Star Matrix gives us a brand new self concept.

If you are only reading this book, and you have not yet begun recovering your own Star Memories and inscribing them into your Book of Stars, you will have to take my word for it that this will be so.

Once you have ten or twenty Star Memories in your Book of Stars, then you will know what that is, how that works – you will have an inkling of that sense of coming home to yourself at last.

A hundred Star Memories in your Book of Stars, and life will have started to become very different.

This is a predictable side effect of Star Matrix, and it happens to everyone who does this.

From my own experience, what has been particularly powerful and life changing is the connections that happen between the Star Aspects of the past, and my ongoing self here and now.

There is a delight in that, a strength in that, which is hard to explain in linear words.

There is also, and I find this particularly important, an unfolding sense of my purpose and destiny in this lifetime.

Each Star Aspect has contributed to that in their own way, and what I am finding is that my life is becoming one unbroken journey.

One journey, one story that is not going to end with physical death. The Star Line continuous on, unbroken, high above all the worries of the day, no matter what they might be.

I had a personal Star Event with the Star Line.

I've known for the longest time that the soul will go on, and that's been a great source of joy and strength to me for the longest time as well.

However, with hindsight I realise that I thought of physical death as a massive catastrophe, something as scary, dangerous and painful as would be giving birth in the Hard. A nuclear bomb going off, incinerating the old life before the next comes into being.

But when I connected with my Star Line, I couldn't even tell where physical death had occurred!

I tried to find it – a big explosion, or a gap in the Star Line, anything – and *it wasn't there*.

That was a huge moment of enlightenment for that aspect; and as is the case with true Star Events, the world has never been the same since.

The experience of that Star Line, entirely unbroken by physical death – I can't even describe how that felt, what that did for me.

Only love remains.

Only love "makes it" to the next level.

Everything else – all the boredom, wheel spinning, trauma, the suffering, the pain, whatever! - isn't just "not important."

It's absent. It's not there. Not a trace of it.

Only love remains.

This one personal experience alone made it all worthwhile to me.

This one personal experience alone made me understand just how important Star Matrix is when it comes to finding a way to reversing the miseries of humanity across the ages.

I coined the slogan for the GoE "Your happiness matters!"

It's extraordinary that we didn't really understand just how important our happiness is.

Now I do, on a whole new level.

Only love remains.

To understand that changes everything.

And still, it cannot be the end of the story, for the story never ends. It is infinite. Our journey towards love, and more love, and still more love, is as infinite as the Great Creative Order itself.

We are all travelling to the stars.

Each one of us has a path all of our own – a Star Line that is as glorious and mysterious as it is delightful and entirely loving in nature.

Beyond that, and together, we are a field of stars ... and they connect, and form a greater matrix still. So much awaits us in the future!

We are Star Beings. We don't have to be afraid.

And best of all, you don't have to take my word for it.

Discover your own Star Memories.

Connect with your Star Aspects.

Become conscious of your own Star Wisdom, found in this lifetime.

The rest becomes an inevitable discovery.

To me, that's the most beautiful feature of Star Matrix of them all.

To Serve & Protect

Star Matrix is still so young, so new – and we're all still learning about its many benefits and features.

The Star Matrix serves us in so many ways, but two especially amazing features became revealed to me only the other day – to serve us, and to protect us.

I had a sension of the Star Matrix as a suit of armour – literally, like being "the knight in shining armour" - with each star not only serving to light up the entire energy system, but at the same time, to protect us from negativity, from criticism, from attempts to oppress us, to take away our power and our energy.

It was beautiful, it was powerful and it was the answer to how to let our energy systems expand, how we can unfold our radiant wings and raise our crown of lights, but to be SAFE and PROTECTED in doing so at the same time.

Many – if not all of us! - have spent a lifetime hiding how amazing we really are because we were afraid of what would happen if we were discovered.

What would the neighbours think?

Would we not attract a flood of starving energy vampires that would eat us up alive?

Would we not stand out too much, and attract those who are determined to stamp out the light wherever they may find it?

Wouldn't it be dangerous in mind, body and spirit to really be … who we were born to be?

The "energy body armour" sension made up of bright suns eclipsed those old fears in an instance.

The more Star Events we have, the more protected we become, in a direct cause-and-effect.

We don't need to be afraid any longer.

That's beautiful, but once more, Star Matrix exceeds all our expectations.

Our Star Matrix doesn't just protect us. If it did just that, wouldn't we be more than satisfied, more than delighted?

There's more …

Every single Star Memory connects us directly to the greatest power in the Universe – the power of LOVE ITSELF.

Every single one becomes a portal through which we are directly plugged into the greatest, most eternal power source there is – and that is how we connect "with the light."

That's how we do that.

Not by following someone else, but by connecting ourselves directly.

- **Every Star Moment opens up a new portal.**

These portals are not islands in an infinite ocean – they are all connected, and the more portals we open, the more powerful the grid becomes.

Now, not only do we not need to be afraid any longer of coming out of the closet as a truly shining being, we can start to become HUNGRY for more Star Events that will make us even shinier!

From hiding in fear in the shadows, we can finally unleash our never ending HUNGER FOR LOVE and seek out consciously new, more, brighter Star Events than we have ever known before!

YES! To more and more Star Events!

Our Star Matrix is here to serve us, to protect us – and to let us move forward now into the future, towards the Future Stars, the Treasures & Riches that are still to come, and will absolutely exceed all our expectations afresh!

The Future of Star Matrix

I want everyone in the world to re-connect to their Star Memories.

We need this – we need empowered people who know their purpose and destiny; who understand themselves and their motives; who actively seek new Star Events of personal enlightenment; who assist others in reconnecting with their Star Memories, with their own true selves.

There are three key features of Star Matrix which must be freely available to everyone, without a payment wall to protect this life saving information, and I encourage you to share this as soon as possible, and with as many other people as you can.

1. Remember the best moments of YOUR life! This is important for your well being in mind, body and spirit, and the more you do this, the more beneficial it becomes.

2. Start your own Book of Stars TODAY! It's YOUR book of life, your magic book, your proof that your life has actually been amazing already, and will get ever more amazing, the older you get.

3. Ask OTHER PEOPLE about their Star Memories!!! This is how true human wisdom, human intelligence, human progress comes into being – learning from each other what is really important about life, so we can live the best lives we can.

This is super simple, super powerful, doesn't require any previous knowledge of anything at all. You don't even have to be able to read and write – you can draw stick figures to represent the Star Event instead, and what an amazing Book of Stars that would turn out to be!

These three instructions will lead to all the inevitable discoveries that we already have, and an inconceivable inpouring of rich information that will lead to amazing new discoveries about what human beings are, and what they can do with their lifetimes on Earth.

If someone wants to know more, and/or is in a position to do more with others, they can buy this book, or attend a Star Matrix workshop, which is quite wonderful with many people understanding how this works, and contributing their Star Memories and experiences to what is an amazing event of human learning.

In the meantime, tell everyone about our three basic ingredients which make Star Matrix work.

I would also invite you to play with Star Matrix and all the people you meet. Tell them about Star Stories, ask them about their Star Stories – and be delighted how easy it was to raise energy of another person, to make them forget their sorrows for a while, start to smile and come to life before your very eyes. It's wonderful – and yet so profoundly simple.

Star Matrix 1ˢᵗ Edition Conclusion

In October of 2019 I couldn't stand it any longer – I absolutely had to finally come forward with something I had known for a very long time by then, namely that our Star Memories are where it's at for this lifetime and beyond.

I ran the first course for Star Matrix beginning on November 11ᵗʰ, 2019 without knowing exactly what the steps in the 12 part program would be, but it had to be done right there and then, and I went ahead.

I used the metaphor of taking a trip to the Stars, on board a Star Ship, to go where literally nobody had ever gone before, and bring back information that nobody had ever tried to assemble in consciousness.

It was scary and it was incredibly exciting too.

The first group of Star Travellers were 40 people from all manner of different backgrounds, with all manner of different problems across the board, but that was of no consequence at all, because we were just going to explore Star Memories in an orderly fashion.

To be fair, I was blown away by the "side effects" from the very first week onward.

My brand new Star People went out immediately and applied the quest for positive memories in the real world.

There was a lady who came across a group of crying women in a hotel lobby who had assembled to celebrate the passing of a friend they had been with for over 30 years. She stepped in and asked about good memories of the dead friend, and transformed the experience for those ladies who were total strangers to her in under five minutes.

Another lady at a traditional family gathering took control for the first time in her entire life and the family gathering turned into the best that had ever been.

Another lady asked her hair dresser for the best thing that had happened to her since last she saw her. The hairdresser was astonished and cried, "Nobody has ever asked me this before!" and, after happy and funny Star Stories were exchanged, and a beautiful high energy hair cut had been achieved, the hairdresser said, "I'll ask all my clients that from now on! I'm so tired of hearing all the complaints, this will be so much better!" This one change could create ripples upon ripples of connection, learning, and happiness, I was so delighted when I heard this!

The stories about re-connecting with other family members, some people had not talked to in decades, were also really amazing.

Star Matrix is the way to connect, to get into deep, loving, positive rapport with people, high energy exchanges that are so, so beneficial for mind, body and spirit!

Especially the stories of speaking to old or very old relatives, in nursing homes, in hospitals, and getting them to smile were truly beautiful to me. Instead of experiencing these interactions as boring, tedious and energy sucking, depressing, to start looking at old people as literally treasure chests full of gold and amazing jewels, and starting to ask for those gifts that only they would have to give, is **a radical transformation in perceiving the value and worth of older people in our society.**

Rather than becoming irrelevant because they don't know how to operate an artificial intelligence interface, the real stories of human enlightenment are there for us to learn from. With a little experience in questioning people, mining people for their Star Jewels, we can even get the exact right Star Stories out of the many which will aid us, right here, right now, in our own personal evolution! This is extraordinary – revolutionary!

Intrapersonally, we have the re-connection between the different aspects of a person across time and space. This has been described as "a sensation of aspects linking hands across my life." As I write this, Star Matrix is not even six months old; so I cannot know at this time what that particular benefit brings over time; but this sense of strong connections between aspects of different ages and in different circumstances is very empowering and curiously magical.

Some people have mentioned that they had an experience of connecting with their ancestors. For some of these, it was entirely surprising and for the first time in their entire life; for others, it was an existing connection lighting up. One person told me, "I always thought my ancestors were a bunch of crazy barbarians and I wanted nothing to do with them. But then the idea occurred that they too must have had Star Events, that the very best of who they ever were is in that Star Space as well. When that idea came, it was as though this entire galaxy of stars lit up behind me, and I felt a powerful sensation of being supported and protected, that my ancestors had my back, for the first time in my life. It was incredibly powerful, a true Star Event in its own right!"

I had known that connecting with high energy aspects and powerful good memories would raise energy and make the energy body happier; still, it was surprising to see that theme of "connection" playing out over and over in all sorts of wonderful ways, bringing insights and ideas, AHA! moments, laughter and smiles.

I had speculated or theorised that if we work with positive memories, it would be easy and fun to remember things clearly, and that is absolutely the case. What I had not expected, and where Star Matrix exceeded my expectations many times over, were the practical side effects of memory improvement.

When I say "memory improvement," I mean the following noticeable changes in how people were remembering in general.

Of course, the first thing was that accessing positive memories became easier, fast. From struggling to remember "anything good about my childhood at all" to getting clear flash backs to happy times when this was requested happened within the first week of the course.

Some people also experienced the Cascades – when it feels like a dam has burst, and a whole collection of memories streams by super fast, a beautiful Star Event in its own right. This is the description of when a blockage in the energy body gives way, and a lot of energy and information literally rushes through its rightful channels at last. Apart from the wonderful feeling and full knowledge that something really important has just happened in the energy system, something was healed in a powerful and natural way, a Cascade also brings with it tremendous insights. They are a beautiful thing, and a version of the Energized End State from EMO, and the Threshold Shift from Project Sanctuary/SuperMind.

But there were other intriguing side effects relating to memory. The clarity of memories improved, and not just of the old Star Memories we were investigating. People were able to remember all manner of other things far more clearly; this was particularly noticeable in some of the older relatives of our participants, who started to remember appointments better, names of people, and where they had left their glasses.

I would very much like to see a host of studies conducted with people suffering from memory loss in various ways and the long term effects Star Matrix has, beyond the improvement in self worth and well being that even the most basic form of remembering your Star Event brings with it.

In that context, there is another area that is highlighted by Star Matrix and this is the "other" Super Powers. It is fascinating that normal people absolutely have memories of doing things that are deemed to be paranormal or supernatural, but clearly, as everyone has these, they can't be "super"natural, but indeed are natural and normal for human beings, if entirely ignored, unreported and unexplored in any meaningful way.

For example, if it happens once that a person gets a clear warning to "step forward" that is so powerful that they can't ignore it, so they step forward, and a piano crashes down into the space they have just moved away from, this means that there is a system that belongs to that person which can do that. By ignoring such memories, we miss out on truly fascinating opportunities to use such Star Memories as a portal to further exploration. Particularly when more people start to talk about those Star Memories, and it turns out that everyone else has memories like that as well, we're dealing with a hugely under-explored system of normal humans that would be really useful if we could learn to activate it in consciousness.

Yes, and then we come to the "better self esteem" or "the brand new self concept" that Star Matrix offers in the advertisements. I know for a fact from long experience that playing to your strengths makes you strong, but it was fascinating to see how that began to show itself in the individuals over the time of the course.

Our trauma/injury directed "victim self" was always wrong, and yet when I proposed Star Matrix for the first time, a lot of people felt terrified that they would change "too much," or that their fragile self concepts would somehow crash and burn, and they would be left … naked and helpless?

What actually happened was that people found their way back to themselves.

I could say, for example, that rather than getting some sort of personality transplant, that "Silvia was always Silvia, and now it turns out that this was actually a good thing, a special thing, something to be proud of, and something that nobody and nothing can ever take away."

This goes back to the "themes" that we find in the Star Memories. There is a structure here, this whole thing isn't as random and chaotic as focusing on the trauma events will lead us to believe.

The Star Matrix makes us more "us" - each one of us.

All these powerful, positive real life memories finally activated and connected makes us ever more "us." And there comes a tipping point when enough Star Memories have been brought to consciousness when the evidence simply becomes overwhelming, and we really have to change our minds then. Or I could say, there is a tipping point where our minds simply change about some very important topics.

For some members of the very first Star Matrix trip, this tipping point came with the Star People.

You simply cannot remember ten, twenty or more incidents where you were significantly helped by another person, and then go on to claim that there was no love in your life, that nobody ever loved you, or that nobody ever cared for you.

The flip side of this coin works in the same way. You simply cannot remember having been a Star Person to other people and beings on ten, twenty or more occasions (Cascade!) and go on to claim that you are nothing but a hapless victim.

It's not possible for a human being to do that. We are surprisingly reasonable and rational by design, and when there is enough evidence, we are built to accept that new truth which is completely different from what we knew before.

This kind of learning, when a dam breaks because the evidence has become too overwhelming to be ignored any longer, is reality learning.

It doesn't go away when we are stressed; it's not just a belief, it's a "the truth."

No matter how stressed you are, you never forget gravity. You practised that as a baby by endlessly dropping toys from your pram until the fact that things fall to earth when you let go off them became a "the truth about this world."

What we discover on a most personal level in Star Matrix is that we were loved; that we did love; that we did have help and protection; that we could do wonderful things.

We discover, each one of us, that we are truly, wonderful beings who had amazing lives already so far.

It's remarkable what that does a person's "self concept" and their "self esteem."

It's a wonderful thing.

By some wonderful mystery, the first Star Matrix course finished exactly as the Global Panic Pandemic of 2020 began. I am so grateful that it did; that my aspects started when they did, so that the first course was complete, clean and tidy, before the onset of a complete cataclysm of normality.

I had set a date for the start of the 2nd course, because I was personally really keen to do this as a participant, without the stress of having to create the course for a change. This was set for April 20th, 2020 (I like to play with numbers!) but by then, we were right into the first weeks of isolation. Should I cancel the course? For a short time, I was doubtful, but then it really came to me that Star Matrix must go on. It is too important for individuals, but also, for at least the Western World itself.

Roger Callahan wrote a book called "End the Nightmare of Trauma."

I've often thought about this, and what he didn't realise was that you don't end the nightmare of trauma by focusing on trauma. This nightmare world of terrible childhoods, mothers and fathers who didn't love us properly, traumatic toilet training, child abuse and all the rest that has totally disempowered people and may even be responsible for the great insanities of our days, from micro-aggression to virulent and toxic divisions between men and women, the generations, different viewpoints that no longer even listen to each other, to trying to fix everything with pills, injections and artificial intelligence – humanity has gone wrong on an epic scale.

This is nothing but energy body stress. We really need to "end the nightmare of trauma."

We need to remember who we really are. We need to stop fighting with each other and start communicating differently. We need to learn to think differently. We need to re-set our goals to love, to the future, to empowerment – we need Star Matrix.

So I am sitting here at my desk, writing the very first Star Matrix book ever.

We are at the absolute beginning of an exploration, of a discovery, of a journey to the stars.

There are no downsides to Star Matrix that I can conceive of.

It is a hugely intimate and personal journey into the real you that starts with the first, most basic attempt to make an inventory of your most meaningful life events.

I have absolutely no idea of what happens when we do this for ten years, or more.

I have no idea what that will do to our brains, our activities, our reality creation, all our relationships, our networks of influence in the long run.

I have a sense of tingling excitement when I consider this, however, and at the same time, a real regret that I didn't have the chance to learn this earlier in this incarnation.

It would be wonderful if young people, children, were taught from the earliest of ages to tune the other way – to tune to Star Events, Star Experiences, and to share their Star Stories with others. There, my dear Energy Minds sends me a scene, of a three year old telling her Star Story to her great grandfather, and him lighting up in response, he seems to glow from within.

Star Matrix has the power to bring more love into the world.

That's a beautiful thing.

But what about all the trauma? All the truth of endless pain and suffering, and the terrible, terrible things humans do to each other? We can't just ignore all of that?

Why not? That's my instant response. That's the old. We've been doing this, on steroids, for what seems like forever. Let's take a trauma holiday in the widest metaphorical sense and focus on the Star Memories, just for a few weeks, a couple of months, and find out what happens to us when we do.

Perhaps we might find that when we return, we have a different take on all the problems.

We will be stronger in ourselves, each one of us; we will have a different appreciation of ourselves, our worlds, and the other humans who live here.

Perhaps we will come back with brand new ideas of healing that were never known before.

Who knows?

I'm smiling as I type this.

More empowered people find better solutions.

This is a fact, a deep principle that we can rely on absolutely.

In my book (r)Evolution, I talk about the "Fish Tank of Insanity," of a world of people being trapped on the negative side of the Modern Energy Chart, behind the massive conceptual wall of ZERO EMOTIONS. No healing can be found there, no intelligence, no wisdom, no love.

I have sought for a reliable, easy way to break free from this conceptual prison, and I sense that Star Matrix is that way.

Please remember our 3 basic steps, for which you need no previous Modern Energy knowledge or any type of "school learning" at all, which are:

1. Start actively remembering your own best experiences, your Star Events, of this life.

2. Start your own Book of Stars to document the evidence.

3. Ask other people about their Star Memories.

That's it.

You can even leave out the first and second step, and just ask other people about the Star Events in their lives.

The more of us do this, the more love, intelligence and wisdom will return to the "world of human beings," and we will have significantly contributed to the evolution of all humanity.

Now, it's over to you.

Get to know you. Remember the very best moments of your life. Write them down in your Book of Stars. And remember to ask other people about their Star Events.

We are all on our journey to the stars.

With all my love, and may your future path be blessed with more Star Events than you ever hoped for,

Silvia Hartmann

Creator, Modern Energy & Star Matrix

Eastbourne, May 1ˢᵗ, 2020

The Journey To Star Matrix: Silvia's Star Stories

Star Matrix is a simple concept, and it confounds me that it's taken so long to get here.

Indeed, it's been a long road – 50 years, half a century, to finally find the "perfect personal development program" that has the power within it to stand up to all the nonsense of the ages and actually works for real human beings.

I feel this book would not be complete without the Star Stories that were particularly responsible for getting me from there to here; and the theory goes that there is always additional, precious information and energy in a Star Story that goes beyond mere words, or lists of techniques.

Of course, there are always many more Star Events involved than we consciously know as yet; the following are the Star Stories my dear Energy Mind wanted to include in this first ever edition of "Star Matrix."

Prequel: The Road Trip With Aunt Annie & Uncle Jupp

How precious, practical and amazing positive memories really are was understood, explored and used for personal gain first of all by an aspect of mine who was perhaps ten years old, and extremely highly strung, as the saying goes.

She was informed one day that a road trip was to take place across Germany, with two elderly relatives, Great Aunt Annie and Great Uncle Jupp. She would be sitting between them for some thousands of miles, and better behave flawlessly, as there was a sizeable inheritance at stake.

Now Aunt Annie and Uncle Jupp were both born in the 1800s, they were childless, very very religious, incredibly strict in every way, and dour of disposition, to say the least. Everyone in the family feared them because they were so difficult to deal with, so demanding, so critical of the tiniest mote of dust, the tiniest wrong doing, the smallest slight, perceived or imagined.

The aspect sighed, took her place between them in the back seat of the father's car, and the road trip began.

And there, the aspect had a flash of pure brilliance. She began to ask them about their childhood experiences, what they were doing when they were ten years old, what games they liked to play, what objects they had that they treasured.

What happened next was nothing short of a miracle.

The old couple started to become animated, told stories; they actually smiled and even laughed out aloud as various tales of mischief and fun were recounted. The aspect asked further and more in-depth questions, to help make the worlds they were telling her about more real "in her mind," and thus began to live in a world before the turn of the 20th century, where the fields were ploughed by huge horses with hairy feet that could stomp a farm child that had no shoes, and where little girls were sent off to work as servants at the same age the aspect was now.

It was amazing. The aspect's parents were totally dumbfounded by what was happening behind them in the car, couldn't understand how the three in the back got on like a house on fire, why the old couple didn't seem to care about crumbs on the seats any longer, why they had stopped complaining, why they were … happy.

It was unknown to see these two be happy.

But there weren't just two – there were three in the back seat.

The third one was expected to be having screaming fits, temper tantrums, to be hugely difficult in her own right, but she was not.

The little girl was living in an extraordinary new world and her questions were being answered, and in fact, there were three ten year olds in the back of that car, just having fun for the entirety of the trip.

It was an amazing experience that was to all intents and purposes, entirely forgotten, apart from a close and happy relationship with the old relatives that lasted until they died.

But eventually, the aspect grew up and got involved with psychology and personal development, where it's all and only about trauma, bad memories – yet, the experience of doing the opposite, the journey into people's positive childhood memories, invented spontaneously by a bored ten year old, was there and it never went away.

Oceans Of Energy

There was a moment in August of 1993 when I had a major Star Event, perhaps the most major Star Event in my life, and I understood how energy works.

In the blink of an eye, all the accumulated evidence of a lifetime, up to then, connected up and I understood how it all works – that energy exists, it's absolutely real, it is being traded between beings and the environment, and that, if you want beings to thrive, you have to provide them with more energy. The whole story of that and other Star Events relating to the genesis of Modern Energy are to be found in "Infinite Creativity," written in 2009, so it doesn't contain Star Matrix as yet.

There were many conceptual pieces missing which were needed to bridge between the Oceans of Energy and the Hard; perhaps the most important of those was the realisation that the 6th Sense is actually our emotions, that it is the energy body which produces them, and that where we feel this through our physical bodies gives us the exact location of where what is happening in the energy body, in a direct cause-and-effect relationship.

This I understood at the moment when a person was crying on the phone because their partner had told them they didn't love them any longer. They complained of "stabbing pains in the solar plexus" and I realised that it was "only energy" - and energy wants to flow! Less than two minutes later, the pain was completely gone, the person was laughing, and the engine behind the practical Modern Energy techniques and systems had come into being, EMO Energy in Motion was born.

With EMO, the wonderworlds of energy could finally be unlocked, and many, many Star Events of all kinds were had, each one contributing to our new field of Modern Energy, which did not come from the ancient mystical scrolls, but **from the real life experiences of many people**.

Yes, and that's one of those miraculous effects of building methods on what real people really feel and do – they work.

It's a wonderful thing!

The Self Healing Energy Body

There was a time in my life when an aspect was very happy. She was freshly in love, work was going amazingly well, she had recovered from a major physical illness and therefore was feeling very grateful to be able to move freely once more; life was great!

There was a bright fresh summer morning, and the aspect got up early, full of beans, and decided to do some hand washing of clothes. She sang to herself, it was fun and easy, then she went into the garden to hang up the clothes into the early morning sunny wind.

She was just enjoying herself when all of a sudden, an old traumatic memory flashed up, moved through and out – and it was gone!

Wow! What was THAT??? What an amazing experience! Instantly, the aspect understood something fundamental – namely that the energy body has a self healing function which is structurally disabled below Zero on the Modern Energy Chart,

The "trauma block" had just bubbled up, then rushed through and out, completely unexpectedly, completely without asking for healing or doing any kind of technique – and the aspect knew it was because she was energy high, and therefore, the energy body had the energy to do some self healing at last.

As with all moments of enlightenment, the information that comes with that is priceless, and essential.

The energy body has a natural self healing ability – of course, just as the physical body has "the power" to mend broken bones, the living energy body has that same ability at the energy levels.

The "self healing" of the energy system gets stronger, more active and more effective, the higher the energy state of a person is.

This explains why "time doesn't heal emotional trauma" when the person who was traumatized remains depressed and in low energy states.

This also explains why time sometimes does heal trauma – especially when a person finds a new love or some other way to make themselves happy.

The "self healing function" of the energy body is just like digestion – it shuts down under stress, doesn't work any more, and when the entire population lives their lives at -4, the very concept of the self healing energy body disappears over the event horizon!

This also revealed the absolute foundational importance of the "energy average" - because the energy average does not just decree how much self healing the energy body can do, but actually decrees what kind of life the person can expect to lead.

The aspect came away from this experience with a whole new understanding of the NEED for higher energy states, why we need to attain them more often, why we need to bring up the energy average itself rather than only focusing on singular events of healing (to try and have them through techniques and sessions, once in a while), which led eventually to the GoE slogan, "YOUR HAPPINESS MATTERS!"

How to PERMANTLY raise the energy average became the new quest from that moment forth.

It was already known how to have high energy events when required (the Healing Event from Modern Energy Tapping, the Energized End State from EMO, the Threshold Shift from Project Sanctuary/SuperMind), that was not the problem any longer.

- **Bringing up the energy average PERMANENTLY was the new goal.**

And eventually, this led directly to Star Matrix!

The End Of The Endless Quest For Trauma

I have told this story many times; it was the turning point for me as far as trying to help people lead a better life by tapping on their traumas of their lives.

Here's what an aspect wrote some years ago:

> I had a client some time ago, a young man who was found at age 6 approximately in a warehouse which had been used by a paedophile ring to make movies.
>
> He was put into care, given a name and birthday as his own was not known, and later adopted by a rich couple. When he became too difficult with the onset of puberty, he was sent back into care; he was abused there too so he ran away. To survive, he then became a prostitute, drug addict and criminal and spent most of his time in and out of prison.
>
> He told me his story in broad brushstrokes, told me about his problems and then asked me, "Can you make me normal?"
>
> I thought about it and then said, "No. Not a chance in hell."
>
> He nodded, laughed and said, "Thank God, at least you're honest ..."
>
> Then, he asked, "So what am I to do?"
>
> And I could feel that energy rising and I said to him,
>
> *"You make sure you have the best life now. The best experiences. Make your life count for something. Pack in as many moments of joy, of grace, of pure happiness as you can.*
>
> *"Then there has to come a time when the Positives outweigh the negatives, and you will have had an amazing life when all is said and done."*
>
> So and instead of delving into any of his innumerable traumas and bad memories, we started working with Positives. To begin with, what he was already good at, what he was proud of. His sensitivity, intelligence, creativity. His strength and the fact that he had never given up. It was an awesome session and he left inspired, delighted, and proud of himself.

It was so simple too. In moments of crisis, he would find a Positive to lift him as he had seen the Energy Chart and understood that he was not "irreparably damaged" but instead, highly stressed all the time, and so life got better for him - of course it did.

Will he ever need to re-visit any of the terrible memories?

Who knows?

That was his past life, and now his life is different.

He is evolving.

This Star Story has two moments which caused a threshold shift in me.

The first occurred when the client asked me if I could make him normal.

I remember clearly that his "trauma life" flashed before my eyes of night, and I was calculating at the speed of light just how many sessions of old negative tapping it would take to make any impact on this man's life, right here and now.

The answer was that it would take INFINITE sessions – absolutely impossible, even if we tapped on traumas for the rest of my life, every single day.

This was what triggered my aspect to exclaim, "Not a chance in hell!"

The second and absolute Star Moment came when he asked, "What am I to do?"

The answer was just there, with that huge up-swell of energy - *__Pack as many moments of joy as you can into your life!__*

This is the right answer, always; and it was a moment of transformation for both me and for the young man. Neither of us ever looked back.

I had not yet arrived at the concept of Star Matrix, that was still to come, but I had understood that trauma wasn't the answer to anything.

The more traumatized a person was, and the more trauma there had been in their lives, the LESS any attempt at trying to treat any kind of trauma could possibly help that person, here and now.

With that also came the insight that "normal" people, who had not been the victim of a paedophile ring, or prostitutes, or abused in care homes, or heroin addicts, or prison inmates, could also not and never be helped by searching for their traumas in a quest to become more empowered, happier.

The whole trauma quest was just WRONG.

This was a huge turning point in my personal quest for self growth as well as my professional quest to find ways to really help people become happier and more successful in life.

I say "turning point" and I mean that literally. "Pack as many moments of joy as you can into your life!" finally took the attention away from the trauma of the past, and placed it on the Star Events of the future instead. The question became instead of, "How to deal with the past?" **"What are we going to do in order to create new Star Events in the future?"**

This turning around and gaining a clear and direct Future Orientation was foundational to all of Modern Energy and the image of a person, walking their timeline, with a few Stars behind but many Stars ahead went into every book and training manual in due course.

What was interesting in hindsight is that it wasn't the past itself that was the problem; it was the focus on past trauma. We don't learn how we create the Future Stars by looking at the trauma; but if we were to look at the past Stars instead, then we would gain valuable information that would help us, put us in a much better position to then experience more Future Stars as well.

This young man's name is in my Book of Stars.

The Golden Jelly In The Sunshine

Not long after my "no more trauma!" experience, I had another client who also believed wholeheartedly that their entire lives had been nothing but failure and misery because he had such a terrible childhood.

This gentleman was particularly hung up on the dreadful neglect he had suffered as a child and was ready with many, many examples of trauma memories of being beaten and abused, treated like a dog.

He had paid for what he entirely expected to be a trauma delving session, but I really wasn't in the mood, so I asked him about a positive childhood memory.

That was the first time I deliberately and actively did that; I was curious and if we can't be delving into childhood trauma, where else could we go?

It was fascinating to observe this gentleman as he raised his eyebrows and stated conclusively that there was nothing whatsoever good about his childhood – it had been an unmitigated hell of abuse and neglect of what he remembered, and anyway he didn't remember anything much from his childhood at all, it was all blank below age 8.

Even though he was extremely convincing, I remember clearly starting to smile on the inside. I have had a very strange childhood myself, with a fascinating collection of abuse of all sorts and then some, but I have always also been aware of the moments of grace that did occur, and I did treasure those, even at a very young age.

No matter how convinced he was, I knew absolutely that he was wrong.

There were good memories there, he was just not accessing them. He didn't know how to access them.

I remember leaning forward, moving into a very interesting energy state, looking deeply into his eyes and saying to him, "You do have good memories. I know you do. The question is only – which good childhood memory will you remember first? Right here, right now?"

He blinked his eyes fast, repeatedly, and then his whole being changed; his mouth fell open and he said weakly, "I remember … something ..."

That was such a moment of wonderment for me, to be and sense this moment with this gentleman, when he remembered …

A very young boy, a very young aspect, perhaps 3 or 4 years old, locked up in his bedroom in a mobile home on site.

The mother and current lover had gone for a party but had not returned; the child was desperately hungry now, a day or two later, and couldn't wait any longer.

The young aspect managed to break open the window, climbed out of it, went round to the entrance, which was not locked, went inside, went into the small galley kitchen, climbed up – but the cupboards were all empty, there was nothing he could eat inside. He felt around on the highest shelf and there came across a packet of cube jellies, stuck to the back. He pulled it free, climbed down, and there was that MOMENT when he ate the orange jellies, radiant in the sunshine, on the steps of the motor home, and experienced blissful happiness.

The gentleman in the here and now with me started to glow as he was retelling this Star Story for the very first time since it had happened, decades and decades ago, and then he couldn't stop talking about how amazing this memory had been, how strong and resilient this small boy had been, how he had figured out how to save himself, care for himself, and how much he admired this child.

I was in deep rapport with him and experienced these extraordinary energy states in my own self as he was having them – here was a real sun rise in the energy system happening right before my eyes!

I tasted the healing power of positive memories for the first time, and I was simply blown away by this.

The gentleman in question was so amazed, so HAPPY, so, so grateful to me, to his past aspect; to have had this experience. He said that one memory changed his life. It changed his mind. It began the most healthy questioning of his long held beliefs about the nature of his life, about his entire existence, and more beyond.

It was a life changing experience for him, and it was also a life changing experience for me.

When this gentleman "remembered," or we could say, when he connected with the experience and the aspect, something magical happened. I always knew that we need more connection between the aspects of our lives, and that there surely, surely must be more than endlessly healing "the wounded child within."

Here, we had made contact with the Star Child within, and the experience was life changing for both client and practitioner. It was so beautiful, so right, so transformational, so healing – and the energy flow had been the other way, from the Star Child to the suffering adult here and now.

We could say that the Star Child had healed the man.

Wow. How beautiful is that? How right does that feel, how glorious the applications, and what potential lies in this not just for healing, but for true evolution and raising the energy average permanently?

This is – magical in its perfection!

But there was a problem.

With all these people, everyone in fact, all being still completely brainwashed into the old trauma trap, how on Earth do you bring POSITIVE MEMORIES into play at all under the established trauma paradigm?

Is it even possible? This is so far away from everything we have ever been taught in therapy, in psychology, in personal development or even spiritual development, how could I bridge this into what was happened all around me still?

At the same time, I knew now that we needed to explore the positive memories. They were precious.

They were … our true treasures and riches.

The Depth Of The Trauma Brainwashing Hell, Revealed ...

In 2009, I created the Modern Energy Chart to make it easier to understand how energy affects emotion, and thereby behaviour.

Until I created this, and its little brother, the SUE Scale (Subjective Units of Experience, Hartmann 2009), the world did not have a scale of POSITIVE emotions. We only had the negative scale, which ends at ZERO – having no emotions at all.

Now this may work for something, what that may be, I couldn't say, but it sure as hell doesn't work for real human beings, who are striving for the Positive, are desperately in need of the Positive, need more love, more energy, more power – every which way you want to call this need for ENERGY that is so rampant in our stress riddled societies.

From 2011 onwards, I was teaching people that you start on the negative side of the chart with a problem, then you have to ADD ENERGY to get onto the positive side. You keep adding energy, and a threshold shift MUST happen – it cannot not happen. This is structural, repeatable, a matter of simple truth, and it is the way to guarantee a healing energy experience. When that has occurred, the problem is solved, it's gone, it never comes back.

This is simple, makes sense, it's reliable – but people weren't using it. They stopped at Zero, didn't even try to push on towards the actual energy body solution which is at +10, they were trapped in the "Fish Tank of Insanity" that ends at Zero, where we are cycling slowly up to Zero, then stop, sink back down into the negative states, and round and round it goes.

I didn't understand this, and kept wondering why oh why people weren't using the Modern Energy Chart as a simple ladder to success – until it came to my experiences with the Energy Tapping course I was teaching at the time.

In this course, there was a full unit on the negative effects of positive memories – the Guiding Stars. Guiding Stars are aborted enlightenment events that don't complete to become a true Star Event; and they cause behaviour to be repeated over and over again in the attempt to finally the event.

This was already known since 2002; Guiding Stars are the direct reason for looping behaviours, such as collections, fetishes, philias and addictions of all kinds; plus they can literally freeze the energy system in a juvenile state, which becomes more and more of a problem, the older a person gets.

Clearly, in trying to solve problems that humans have, the Guiding Stars are of supreme importance, far more important than trauma, because trauma teaches us what to avoid, whereas Guiding Stars drive forward behaviour of DOING something over and over, that may very well be not in a person's best interest.

So in this course, and in the Unit on Guiding Stars, there was the exercise at the end - "Find and evolve an event of your own."

I had deliberately phrased it like this, in order to catch out the student or two who would miss the point of the Unit, and instead of finding and treating a Guiding Star, would run straight back into a trauma of some kind.

This was a correspondence course, and I had 197 people on it, from literally all walks of life, all sorts of countries, old, young, all levels of education, all kinds of different religious affiliations.

When the first student came back with the story of how they treated a trauma, I laughed. I sent them back to do a Guiding Star instead.

But then, the 2nd and the 3rd student did the same. They also treated a trauma.

By the time over 20 students had all treated yet another trauma, I stopped laughing and started to get scared.

When every single one of the 197 students, and there were many among them which I would consider to be highly experienced in Modern Energy, 197 out of 197 ALL rushed straight back into trauma I had truly understood how deep and profound the trauma brainwashing of the Western World really was.

It was shocking. It was horrific. The aspect understood right there and then that it wasn't enough to show people the Modern Energy Chart and the SUE Scale.

The positive wing of these scales, the entire land of "health and happiness" was a totally unknown country to them. It was absent from their conscious beliefs; it was absent as goal, it just wasn't there.

I understood that I needed something much more powerful than just the clean logic and perfectly replicable information from the Modern Energy Chart.

I needed something that could break the spell that had bound the Western World for a hundred years and more, not just in therapy, but actually, in song, in movies, in tales, in stories, in everything – it's all trauma, all the way.

Thus began the quest for something so powerful, so incontrovertible, that it could break the "curse of psychotherapy." I needed to find something new, a totally different way to do both personal healing as well as personal empowerment on a grand and fundamental level.

Understanding Memories

In 2013, I gave the very last live Energy EFT training ever, in Baltimore, in the US of A.

This was the same training that, in 2011 as a correspondence course, had unmasked the depth of the trauma entrainment, and I wasn't going to play that game any longer.

The course itself dealt with how to help other people get over their problems, and of course that would involve trauma tapping, what else could there possibly be, and the participants of course eagerly expected to be able to tap for three days straight on all of their own many traumas.

Unfortunately for all of us, I had it with trauma by then, fully, thoroughly, deeply and profoundly.

Foundational to this course is to understand how energy body events create memories.

But my aspect did not go into trauma memories to teach this.

She chose to ask for positive memories instead to teach the principles.

And that was utterly revolutionary.

It turned out that positive memories are radiant, resonant, so clear, so perfectly present in all six senses, they were super easy to deal with.

Not just that, the structure of how events work, how they create meta comments that form our "beliefs" about reality was so obvious, so clear to track as a pattern, it was amazing.

With hindsight, I think of it like this.

Trying to discern the structure of memory by working with trauma memories is like trying to discern the reality of a frog by studying a frog that had been repeatedly run over with a steam roller, and is nothing but a distorted green, red and oozing mess now.

There's no life in it. You can't even tell what was the skeleton and what was the skin.

There is just no way you can learn anything at all about a living frog that way.

Working with the radiant, resonant, steady, lucidly 3D clear POSITIVE memories was clearly the way to go.

I understood right there that a person should know how to work with their own memories BEFORE they ever, ever, ever get to go near any trauma memories – if they ever need to do that at all, which remains under advisement.

And how and where do you learn how to access memories, gain information from them, walk around in them, connect with the aspects and so much more?

In your high positive memories, of course, and absolutely nowhere else!

I already knew that connecting with positive memories could be healing, life changing, incarnation saving.

Now I knew that to even understand memory at all, and learn how to use it correctly, only positive memories could possibly be the right way to go.

Modern Energy Art Solutions

In my earliest EMO explorations, which were absolutely fascinating and probably contained the highest incidence of Star Events, one after the other, of any stretch of my life so far, I came across Art Solutions.

I was visiting with an artist friend of mine, who always painted the same picture when left to his own devices. This was a self portrait in red and black, featuring a Christian Cross for the eyebrows and nose, with a bloody Jesus hanging from it.

Everybody knew he was painting those, which got consecutively bloodier and more disturbing as the years had gone by, because he had been sexually abused by a catholic priest as a young boy.

This artist was an interesting and creative guy who also could be amazing fun to be with, to be sure; so on this day, my aspect went to visit him at his studio and found him violently stabbing at yet another canvas with yet again the self same horrible picture on it.

As she stepped into the studio and saw this scene, the aspect had an instantaneous enlightenment event – she instantly realised just how bad and wrong it was what was going on here, and wanted to yell, "STOPPIT!" but an energy shift happened and she found herself shouting, **"You're painting the problem – why don't you paint the SOLUTION????"**

The artist friend stopped, turned around, eyes wide open. "The solution? But how? I don't know … how???"

And my aspect shouted back, "I don't know! If the solution had a colour, what colour would it be?"

The friend stood, mouth open, just for a moment, then he began to shout, "It would be blue! Blue!!!"

He shoved the old canvas off the easel, grabbed a fresh one, and moments later, he was putting a sky blue colour with great sweeps of the brush on the top right hand corner of the painting – I was totally forgotten, but that was alright, for I was having my own enlightenment event right there and then – that's where we've been going wrong all this time!

160

We've been painting the problem, over and over, when we should have been painting the solution!

This is EMO Art Solutions, and it's so fundamental to Modern Energy, it literally changed everything.

The very first public change was to switch to what was then called Positive EFT – pure Art Solutions in principle.

You have a problem? Doesn't matter what it is. What (energy) do you need right now to solve it?

Well … I might need a miracle … Great! That's our 1st Positive. We tap a sequence on that, and then we ask again, "And what else do you need to solve the problem?" We keep going up the Energy Chart until there is a threshold shift, a +10 healing event has occurred and the problem is solved.

Simple. Beautiful. Applicable to every problem there is. Let's remember, we're talking about energy body problems here, I am the Energy Guy, to be sure.

Please note, there is no need to "paint the problem" when you apply Art Solutions.

No need to re-visit any trauma at all. From (energy body) problem to (energy body) solution in direct, future orientated steps. It's easy. All you need to know is where to tap, and to ask, "What is the first thing you need to solve this problem?"

Now, the engineer who made EFT, Gary Craig, states unequivocally that "if you tap on Positives, it's not EFT," so we had to change the name of this way of tapping, and it became Modern Energy Tapping instead.

So now, and asking that question, "What do you need to get over problem X?" we were directly working with The Power of the Positives for the first time.

Unfortunately, and because of that massive trauma brainwashing, the vast majority of the EFT "community" didn't get it, didn't like it, didn't try it, wanted nothing to do with it.

That's understandable.

I knew we needed something more powerful, and thus, the quest continued.

Still, I learned many things about "The Power of the Positives" during the research for this.

A real Star Moment occurred when I realised that just writing down lists of Positives would raise energy so significantly. You may think that is fairly obvious, but there was a moment when an aspect had just completed another list of Positives for people to tap on to go into the Positive Tapping book, got up from the computer to make a drink and found that there was no gravity!

I'm laughing as I'm writing this; the aspect didn't exactly float to the ceiling but felt so light, movement was like dancing; and as though she could spin on the spot and touch the entire world, all at once.

After the initial outburst of joy, she realised that by doing nothing more than typing down a list of highly energizing words, such as Diamond Energy, Sapphire Energy, Ruby Energy, Aquamarine Energy, Amethyst Energy, she had raised her own energy state not just into the high positives, but had actually triggered a Plus Ten state, quite inadvertently.

I would say that this was the genesis of "The Power of the Positives" - to understand that any interaction with energy forms that are experienced as highly positive for a person really has the power to heal and transform that person. That there is an endless reservoir of powerful, powerful energy gifts which you can unlock by simply thinking about them, or writing them down in a list. It just could not be easier and yet more profound if we tried.

Essentially, this Star Event of floating after doing nothing more than writing down a list of Positives was the "end of tapping as the be all and end all."

Tapping is a great self help method, don't get me wrong; but it's not the only way to raise energy reliably, and I had seen far too many good people over the last couple of decades getting totally "stuck on negative problem tapping," which is clearly not a good thing when you want some serious evolution to occur.

This experience with the list of precious gemstone energies also opened the door to taking the "Personal Power Positives" far more seriously.

The Personal Power Positives

This is a pivotal moment in the genesis of Star Matrix we have reached here.

Where do you get a "Personal Power Positive" from?

What could possibly be a Positive that is unique to a person, and immensely, instantly empowering?

Well … perhaps you could get such an energy form, expressed as a word, or a concept, from a high positive memory such as the "Orange Jelly In The Sunshine!"

I decided to build that pattern into the first ever Modern Energy Tapping Pro Training, which is entirely based on healing problems using The Power of the Positives.

> *Do you remember a time when an aspect was walking on water, unstoppable, completely in the zone? Tell me the story …*

The first time I taught this, someone told me of an experience when they were young and running bare foot over dry grassland, in an undulating landscape of low hills, as the sun was rising. They said it felt like they were flying, but at the same time, owning all the land, and moving forward not just across the land, but across time itself, with perfect speed.

I asked them to sum up this Star Experience with a short phrase that would become their "Personal Power Positive," and they said, "Perfect Speed."

It was exquisite to watch the person change their state as they were telling me of this memory. Their energy changed, of course, but so did their entire body – they straightened up, started to smile, to glow, became … liquid, in motion, before my eyes.

This immediately connected up with my own experience writing down that list of Positives – this person was "getting energy high" just by recalling that experience, and by giving it a conscious title, they had gained "a handle on it."

There was also neither need or desire to tap on "Perfect speed" whatsoever. The state change had been accomplished purely by a) remembering, b) telling the story of the experience, and c) giving the experience a title.

That last step, finding a way to "name" the experience, was the final CLICK! the entire person had needed to put the whole thing together.

It was as though once the consciousness also understood, had a handle on that memory, had a name for it, everything was present that needed to be there to cause what was a transformational energy event in its own right.

The person was extremely energy high; so was I; and they told me how utterly amazed they were that they could be in their own time and at their own speed like that; they always thought they were totally out of sync with their own time and everybody else's time as well.

They couldn't stop talking about how amazing this was, how life changing, how precious to understand that, and thanked me most profoundly for this experience.

And all I had done was ask them to tell me the story of a time when they were in the zone …

Now I could have made my stand on Modern Energy Tapping[2]; bought lots of advertising for it and concentrated on it, because it's actually really beautiful, but I was and am on the quest for the extraordinary, for something that could really, really make a difference, and with this person at the first MET Pro training, there it was once more – **the positive memories in and of themselves deserved attention, so much more attention than they had ever received before.**

---

2 "Modern Energy Tapping – Engage The Power Of The Positives!" Silvia Hartmann, DragonRising 2016

The Movie Star Experience

A huge part of the whole "Journey to Star Matrix" exists in the Modern Energy Art developments, and a personal breakthrough of previously unknown proportions awaited the aspects there.

In 2017, I decided to offer a comprehensive course on Modern Energy Art (MEA for short) as an online course. It soon became clear that folk couldn't be taught this with still pictures and writing, and that they needed to see me do this and explain it on video.

But my aspects were HIGHLY reversed to having their picture taken, or being filmed. There is good reason for this and a well known pit of endless childhood trauma – yet, the MEA course would not work without it. The aspect had to get over it somehow.

At the bottom of the garden is the studio on my property, originally built for sound recording. This is where the recording of the MEA videos was to take place, and the poor aspect stood, looking down the garden path, feeling very reversed and miserable at the proposition.

What Positive can help me here get over this, once and for all???

And the answer just exploded into the aspect's mind, body and spirit – *MOVIE STAR*!

Just for a moment, the then 58 year old, overweight aspect had a total WTF moment – but then exploded into laughter, laughed so much, she was crying, and on the garden path projected saw the Hollywood Walk of Fame style stars, going all the way into the studio.

This moment changed – everything. Well! A real Star Event does that, it changes your life, and life is never the same again after that.

The aspects recorded the MEA videos, all 24 of them, without any further ado. The experience unlocked the ability to do live social media streams, and make all manner of videos to share her knowledge with others. Further video courses were now available, and not just that – making videos was FUN. Exciting! Always had that connection of sparkles to that original MOVIE STAR! experience.

Now there are so many things about this one Star Event, so many repercussions.

The No. 1 realisation was this.

- **Just ONE really good Star Event has the power to change your life.**

MOVIE STAR proved this without a shadow of a doubt.

Getting people to have **just one Star Event of their own** would make any course of instruction of any kind worth more than my weight in gold - thrice.

Basing a course around having just a single Star Event, and throwing the book of Modern Energy at it, offering a huge variety of exercises so that everyone would have the best chance there would be that one exercise that would trigger their own Star Event, was the next step.

That idea completely shifts how you would construct a course, how to target it, even how you sell it.

With hindsight, this also explains why people go to workshops. They are hoping to have a Star Event there.

This realisation immediately also brought the old "nightmare of trauma" problem to the surface, yet again. Going to a workshop and hoping for trauma healing, and for this, we have to dig up a trauma (problem) first of course, makes it actually really unlikely that any of the participants will have Star Events, because you're going down before you're going up, rather than going straight up all the way.

If you want Star Events, going into trauma isn't the right direction to be going in - metaphorically, consciously, practically, energetically – it's just exactly the wrong way to go.

And if you don't go into trauma, where do you go …?

But for now, we had the idea to make a course that does its absolute best to make it so that the participants each will have a Star Event of their own.

In what context do people need a Star Event to help them literally "change their stars" and change their lives for the better?

As I was musing this, someone contacted me and whined in a text message that would have been 3 A4 sheets if you printed it out (without line breaks, at that!) how they would love to do a course with me but didn't have any money, and they were so poor, and couldn't get any money and and and and.

I looked at that and went, RIGHT! That does it! How many times have I heard this? "I would love to buy your book for ten dollars ... but it's soooo expensive ... and I just can't afford it ... "

We're going to try that new found idea of offering a variety of energy techniques so that people can have that ONE Star Event that will change their lives for the better, take their lives to the next level, and it's going to be the GoE MONEY!!! Course![3] Whoohoo!

I am really connecting to the excitement of the aspect at the time, and the GoE MONEY!!! course is really a most awesome thing. No other aspect but the one who created that could have done it with such power and conviction; it's a brilliant showcase for all things Modern Energy.

Yet and afresh, I knew this **still** wasn't it.

It was on the right track, and the idea that a single Star Event can change a person's life for the better, and that's what we are aiming for or should be aiming for, in any personal development product, ever and always, was right, brilliant, and the next step forward to what I was really seeking – the ultimate personal development product/method/pattern, something that would end the Freudian nightmare, something that had the power to do that.

As I was demonstrating the many different exercises on the MONEY!!! Course videos, of course I had my own energy experiences along the way.

Interestingly, the most intense AHA! came along when members of the first course, which I always do personally so I can learn from the responses of the participants, started to hit the exercise which asked them about a high positive memory in the MONEY!!! context, to inspire them now.

The Star Stories the participants told were amazing.

My own Star Memories were just as amazing

So inspiring, so exactly the antidotes to negative money related energy states – it was beautiful.

And here the two finally connected up.

1. **You only need <u>one</u> Star Event to change your life.**

2. **We have a treasure trove of exactly such Star Events inside of us already!!! Who knew!!!**

---

3   The GoE MONEY!!! Course can be found at <u>GoE.ac/MONEY</u>

This brought me to No. 3, and this would be:

3. If we want to learn how to have more Star Events, surely the clues to how to have them are in the Star Events we've already had!

Here now, the connection was made between the absolutely fundamental and non-negotiable law of Modern Energy, that of the "Future Orientation," and the memories of the past.

The fact is that the past has been and gone. We are here and now, and before us lies the future.

In all natural systems, there is what I call "the grand procession" - the multiverse unfolds, is on a journey, stands never still, it's like a dance where everyone moves along into the future.

In the Hard, we have become detached from that and the Hard is not in step with the grand universal procession. It has weird ideas of "time," doesn't understand "space," and people are constantly terrified of time passing, trying to turn back the clock, trying to stop the natural flow of unfoldments in every way they can, and this is incredibly stressful. Remember raising the energy average I talked about earlier? To get back in sync with the grand universal procession would surely be a huge step in the right direction for human beings!

How does dwelling on past Star Events contribute to that Future Orientation???

Gathering In The Harvest

This needed to be resolved, and it was resolved one fine day when I found a work of art an aspect had created in 2003, based on an Energy Mind derived sension - "Harvesting From The Tree Of Lights."

In a flash, I understood that our Star Memories are indeed, the Treasures & Riches of our lives.

In a flash, I remembered the plane crash survivors who only remembered their Star Events, and nothing else.

In a flash, I understood the meaning of what my Energy Mind had sent me decades ago – the tree is our life, and the lights are the high positive memories.

And the voice said, **"It's time to start gathering in the harvest ..."**

Wow! That was a Star Event in its own right.

I had understood how it all worked, and how the Future Orientation is served by activating our Star Memories in consciousness.

First of all, connecting with Star Memories energizes us immediately, right here and now. It's the easiest and most direct pathway to gaining a sense of empowerment at will. Much faster than any other energy technique there is. Or was. Ever.

Secondly, the Star Memories contain the most information of any memory.

We absolutely NEED this information in order to plot a course for the future. This is the exact information each one of us needs to figure out what we have to do next.

The Star Events are the step stones on a personal path that has a trajectory into the future – they are exactly what we need to get the Future Orientation back.

I understood further (all in that flash moment of seeing the old painting afresh!) that we must spend a time positively discriminating and recovering the Treasures & Riches of our lives, which had been so totally ignored in the Hard.

I knew we must focus now with all speed and as soon as possible on our Star Memories, to take an inventory of what is already there, and to start "gathering in the harvest" - actually making use of all we've learned so far.

I understood perfectly that the path to having more Star Events in the future was to connect with and download the information from the Star Events of the past.

The personal instruction book and field guide to "how to have Star Events" is to be found there, and nowhere else.

Yes, and then, there was the MirrorMan.

The MirrorMan

Around 2005, I was playing with a different version of "Past Life Regression" which was still popular back then, but not something I wanted to be involved in. I asked my dear Energy Mind about this, and it gave me a HypnoDream: "Many Lives In The Multiverse." Shortly after this, I felt moved to make The MirrorMan, and I thought that it might be an overbeing, and each facet would be a life.

This may well be so; but in the autumn of 2019, one day I was walking past my MirrorMan and it flashed into my awareness, as the light struck it – and that was the Star Moment when I got it that **a self concept based on Star Events would be … a Star Matrix.**

Wow.

That was something else.

I had not considered what would happen once you start connecting the Star Events. I had understood the Star Line – a timeline high up where "only love remains." Beautiful.

But I had not thought about what kind of being would be travelling along that Star Line, who that would be, how that would be on a personal level.

A self concept made from the Star Aspects …

Incontrovertible, because it's based on that one person's real life experiences

Indestructible and unassailable.

OMG …

Now wouldn't that be a fine self concept for a person to have …

It may sound impossible, and yet all my own life's experiences led me here, and I knew it was right.

- **The Star Matrix is the <u>only</u> correct self concept for a human being to be having.**

It's essential for a conscious human being to have their own Star Matrix to hold them together and allow them to function correctly.

All of that in a flash.

Star Matrix had its name.

And the whole story about the Star Events just took a massive threshold shift into a whole new dimension of … yes, urgency.

That's the right word.

I've been looking for some way to get people out of stress and up the Modern Energy Chart.

Star Matrix is that way.

I knew it there and then, and from then on, called Star Matrix "my legacy project."

Star Matrix 1 & 2: The Surprises (And The Benefits!)

We have caught up now to the 2019 aspect who announced to the GoE Members that we had a new project – Project 11 as it was called, and then, once the Star Event with the MirrorMan had happened, Star Matrix.

My aspects were hugely excited about it and also quite a bit afraid.

You don't have to worry whether people will enjoy themselves on a Star Matrix course. That's a given. Ask people about their own best memories, and you can't go wrong. You literally cannot go wrong with that. It's impossible. That in and of itself is really remarkable if you stop and think about it for a moment.

The reason my aspects were afraid, and I am still afraid, is that Star Matrix is so other than anything else we've ever done in personal development, that I can't do it justice.

The potential for Star Matrix is beyond what I can conceive. It's … huge. It goes far beyond just remembering a few happy memories, but even if it did just that, it would still be incalculable what would happen if more people did this. How it would spread to other family members, their friends, strangers they met along the way ...

But it's so much more than just that. When you think you got a handle on just how much more, something else happens that blows your mind and makes it even more still.

My own first Star Event with the Star Matrix course came one month into it, at the Christmas party with my ex-husband.

It was my own first personal example of what the aspect called then "Star Matrix thinking" - which is just so different from how I "normally" think, it's mind-boggling. Once more I cannot conceptualise what that will do in the long term, for me or for anyone else who has this happen to them – and then in combination, as people connect and combine …

My second Star Event was the memory flash back to the supermarket scene to explain why the milk had been forgotten. My partner and I were home, unpacking the shopping, when he exclaimed, "There is no milk! I can't believe it! How can we have forgotten the milk???" - and in direct response, instantly, I flashed back to the supermarket, standing in front of the chilled section, watching my partner opening the glass door, about to reach in, and a shop assistant appears. My partner asks her something, and they have a conversation. I can hear perfectly what they are saying, the recall is so clear and bright, I can even read the name badge on the shop assistant's chest. They finish their conversation, he closes the door and walks away – and that's the answer to "How we forgot the milk."

Boy oh boy! I've always had a good memory but that was … what they call "photographic memory," only it wasn't just photographic, but a full on 6 sensory experience of everything that was present at the time. That was absolutely a "side effect" of having practised with the Star Memories for a few weeks by then, and truly amazing to me. I loved it, and I feel we need a new word now – how about lucid memories instead of just photographic memories? Sounds good to me!

My third Star Event involved a "mental movement" that just astonished me. Something triggered an old trauma memory that had been flashing up for 50 years by then, reliably, every time a trigger was presented, and on this occasion, when the memory flashed up, a second memory of a high positive event in the same context, from the same year, flashed up brighter, closer, and moved across to literally eclipse the old memory.

This happened spontaneously, without me asking for it or doing any kind of technique, in the middle of mundane activity in the Hard.

Isn't that the holy grail of trauma resolution right there and then?

I have no idea how that one event will impact my future. It was related to receiving gifts, which had that trauma memory attached for half a century, and now, it has a Star Memory attached to it instead. What will that do??? I have no idea, but I'm certainly keen to find out!

Only a week or so after this happened to me, I was contacted by a member of the first Star Matrix crew who had something amazing to tell me. This person had been "stuck on" a traumatic memory for over 20 years which involved seeing a loved one, covered in blood, dead, after an accident. Since then, this scene would flash up every time a memory of the loved one was triggered, and had been exhausting as well as entirely resistant to every conceivable form of therapy. On this day, the Star Matrix person had simply sat in the garden and asked their dear Energy Mind for the perfect Star Memory to cheer them up – and received a Star Memory involving the loved one, from **before** the accident! They reported a very similar experience to mine – the Star Memory was closer, much, much brighter, more radiant in every way and the old trauma flash back disappeared! Then they experienced an entire cascade of positive memories, flooding in. They were so happy, they danced and cried and felt so, so blessed that they had their good memories back at last, but also, that this had happened without them doing anything other than asking for a Star Memory that would make them feel better on that day. This is really quite extraordinary and yet I've seen this happen before.

Nearly 20 years ago, I was sitting at a bar in a hotel where one of the old style Energy Psychology conferences were being held, talking to a Vietnam veteran, who was seeking help with a traumatic memory which had been haunting him for decades. He had tried "tapping on it" with numerous leading lights of the Energy Psychology scene, but it had not shifted. I remember clearly that the aspect thought, "If he's been treated by all these people, and the trauma isn't shifting, there must be some good reason for that. Perhaps something is protecting that memory, perhaps it's important in some way ..." The idea occurred to ask the man about a positive memory of that time, and he told one – of being with his group in the jungle, night, pouring down with rain, absolutely exhausted, with his head on a comrade's shoulder, and having an experience of being one with all his comrades, and loving them so much, it was beyond anything he'd ever experienced. This had also happened before the traumatic incident; and although I didn't test this, there was a huge, huge sense that something remarkable had happened at the time, and I've thought about this ever since. Many years later I used the same pattern with another veteran, from a different war, and that "eclipse effect" of the powerful positive memory on the old traumatic memory was present there also.

There is much still to be discovered about the practical uses of our high positive memories, and the potential for true life healing to be found there – we are at the very beginning of gathering in the harvest ...

A particularly profound Star Event happened during one of the Star Matrix Masters Candidates interviews, when a participant burst out into tears, thanking me for having given them the tools to make their dying mother happy.

Wow. I have mentioned this many times already, but the potential of (re)connection with family and friends across time and space is once more one of those Star Matrix variables that makes it incalculable in just how much good it could do if only more people knew about it.

Then there was the Star Line moment, where I understood that I don't need to be afraid of death itself any longer. Oh, I have no words how healing that was, how much fear and pain that took away that I never even knew I had been carrying still.

The most recent personal Star Event I had was also spontaneous and to me, totally mind-blowing.

I was doing nothing in particular, gardening in isolation, and the thought occurred to me that I had never wanted anything to do with my ancestors; one of those post 2nd World War generational things.

But what if one connected only with the highest positive aspects that all the ancestors surely must have had? Their Star Aspects?

As I thought this, an entire field of stars exploded at my back, an incredible sensation that pushed me forward so I had to take three steps to regain my balance.

Amazing. That the day would come and I – me, Silvia Hartmann! - would connect willingly with all the ancestors, well that's one I would never, ever have believed possible.

But it happened. And it's in my Book of Stars.

Star Matrix 1 took place before the global panic pandemic of 2020; Star Matrix 2, the second course, landed smack in the middle of fear, panic, and house arrest.

The two courses could not have been more different; the stress states of the participants on the 2nd journey were much worse. And yet, Star Matrix prevailed. In fact, the course became a sanctuary of sanity, of remembering what's important in life and what isn't, and significantly helped some participants with personal tragedy and bereavement.

There was one moment that was once more, personally transformational for me. In the Unit on the Star People, a participant had remembered right away a lovely lady, who had been her matron when a young, frightened aspect first began her nursing career. This lady had been kind, supportive and a fantastic role model for the young nurse. The Star Matrix student felt moved to try and find out if this lady was still alive as she would have to be in her high 80s now; the student tracked her down, and somewhere in the world, a very old lady received an unexpected phone call from a student of her own, from over 50 years ago, who was telling them how much they had meant for their life, how grateful they were, and that they had placed their name in their Book of Stars.

When I heard this, I had a most extraordinary energy sensation, a Star Event of my own, and I knew that I had changed the world.

Now please understand that this, for me, goes back so far that it feels like millennia. I've always, always wanted to change the world, and have done my best for half a century, and of course, there are many instances of such happenings that I am aware of.

But it had never felt real – until that morning and that lovely old lady who had received her phone call, and if I had not been here, doing what I do, that would never have happened.

I did change the world. The burden I never knew I was carrying all this time lifted, and there is a lightness that wasn't there before. This only happened about a week ago as I write this, and the long term repercussions are as yet, unknown. I am so grateful to this experience, and the dear student who told me about what they had done, as well as the lovely old lady who received her phone call, are both in my Book of Stars now.

That is the story so far.

As I write this, Star Matrix is only nine months old.

It is, however, the accumulation of a lifetime's worth of experience with people, and me finally figuring out how to do it right.

I can't conceive of what my life would have been if someone had encouraged the three year old aspect to start their own Book of Stars.

> *"Draw pictures, little Silvia. When you can write words, write words. Only your best memories go into your Book of Stars. And when it's full, you start a new one.*
>
> *"When an aspect of you is as ancient old as I am, they will love all your Books of Stars so very very much!*
>
> *"And they will send their love and admiration across time and space to you, and you will never be alone, you will always be loved, and protected, in many more ways than you can ever know ..."*

As they say, it's never too late to have had a brilliant childhood.

We can create missing events in Sanctuary with consummate ease, at any time we choose.

We are truly, multidimensional beings living in a multidimensional multiverse.

We are but children in this amazing multiverse, and we're still learning to find our ways here.

As I write this, I have just scheduled a 3rd Star Matrix course, to start on September of 2020. I have never in my life run the same course 3 times back to back, I've never, ever wanted to – quite the contrary!

Star Matrix really is my legacy project, the result of 56 years in conscious personal development. It's a thing of beauty, and what I've been looking for my whole life long.

The aspect was right who wrote, "You find yourself at +10."

That's the only place big and wide enough to get a notion of who each one of us truly is.

Star Matrix takes all the +10s and links them up together, without prejudice.

Now, I would say,

> *"Star Matrix is where you find yourself.*
>
> *"Your Star Matrix is the true you – and it is still evolving, will never ever cease to evolve, nothing can stop it. No trauma, not physical sickness, not death itself – you are AMAZING, and <u>I can prove that.</u>*
>
> *"Look to your own Star Memories.*
>
> *"That is your first mirror, your first portal to the best mystery there is – who you are."*

I hope you enjoyed this first journey into your Star Matrix; I certainly loved sharing it with you.

Life is wonderful.

And when life sucks, I laugh and say, "I'm starting to look forward to the afterlife!"

Addendum

Quick & Easy Ways To Raise Energy & Perform Better!

Literally everything works better when we are energy richer, higher on the Modern Energy chart.

"Everything" includes all the exercises in the Star Matrix book, of course :-)

Here is a selection of energy raising exercises to practice, and find your favourites that will work reliably to put you at +5 or above for the best results.

1. The Heart Position – The Treasure Hunt

Assume the Heart Position and breathe in and out, deeply.

Think about the fact that you are going to get a new Star Memory in a moment, and that this will be wonderful, surprising and delightful; that it will help you on this day, and on your way!

You are going treasure hunting – what will you find today?

Let the sense of excitement build with every breath you take until you are ready to go.

2. The Heart Position – Breathing In The Positives

Assume the Heart Position and this time, breathe in Positives, and breathe out stress.

What is the first Positive you need right now to get higher?

Breathe in "Serenity" (or Love, Joy, Destiny, pure Life Force Energy or whatever you crave right now) and breathe out all the way.

You can breathe in the same Positive three times if you are very stressed before moving on to the next one.

Note how you start to feel better and continue until you feel empowered, charged and ready to go.

3. The Heart Position – Find Something To Love

This pattern is particularly good for when we are in very energy poor states and can't think of a first Positive because of stress.

Love is the greatest "stress healer" there is, and thinking about someone or some thing you truly love will spin up your Heart of Energy and raise your state reliably and beautifully.

Once you feel you can think again, you can switch to using Positives (No. 2) to get higher.

4. A Round Of Applause!

Clapping and cheering raises energy fast and high.

Give yourself a round of applause to get from being slightly energized to highly energized in just a couple of minutes.

You can also clap and cheer the beautiful Universe, or anything else that brings you joy to raise energy in this way.

5. Modern Energy Tapping With A Single Powerful Positive

Modern Energy Tapping is a reliable "go to" method to raise energy with the Power of the Positives. Choose a Positive that will help you get higher and tap or touch the energy points whilst speaking the Positive out aloud.

6. Modern Energy Tapping – Empowering A Positive

Creating variations on the Positive on each point makes this more interesting and flexible still. For example, we may start with POWER as the Positive, and the next point will be Mind Power, the next after that Beautiful Power, followed by Infinite Power and so on.

7. Modern Energy Tapping – The Stairway To Plus 10

We can raise even more energy by coming up with a Positive for every single point which will create a sequence of Positives that act like a stairway to +10.

For example, the 1st point could be EXCITEMENT, followed by DISCOVERY, then JOY, BLESSINGS, LOVE ... and so on until all the points have been tapped.

8. EMO Energy Dancing

Here, we make the Set Up to use the physical body to bring more energy flow to the energy body.

We ask our hands to start making movements that will improve energy flow; then ask our wrists, elbows and shoulders to join the dance. This is followed by the head and neck, all the spine, the hips, knees, ankles and toes until the whole physical body is dancing with the joined aim to get the maximum energy flow through the energy body.

Feels fantastic, doesn't require music, and with practice is the fastest way to raise the most energy simply by moving your body even slightly.

A General Note About Energy & Performance

Be aware of your energy management in general throughout your day and night.

I was coaching a group of authors at one time, and it turned out that many among them were attempting to do their writing AFTER EVERYTHING.

By this I mean after everything else that any human being could possibly be doing had already been done, from housework to a full day's work outside the house, childcare, giving partners, other family members and friends all their attention; after the pets had been groomed and fed; the houseplants been watered, and literally everything else had been done – and then they sat down and expected to be creating great writing.

Many people in personal development do the same thing. In their list of priorities, born out in their actual behaviour in the real world, meditations or exercises are placed AFTER EVERYTHING ELSE, into a zone where they are mentally, physically and spiritually drained.

This pattern guarantees poor performance and pathetic results. Obviously.

Turn it around, and put the activity in question BEFORE EVERYTHING, by getting up an hour earlier if necessary and getting (the writing, the meditating, the Star Memory exercises!) done before everything else kicks off, we get results that are not just exponentially better every single time, but a vast, vast improvement overall as these better performances built our abilities and understanding so much faster and better together.

By putting our personal development activities BEFORE EVERYTHING, we also make a clear statement to mind, body, spirit and whoever else will listen and give us a hand that whatever it is we want to accomplish here by doing this in the first place is IMPORTANT!

We do personal development to have a better life, to create a better life for ourselves and those we love. Wouldn't it be nice if it actually started to work, and even nicer if it started to work on a whole new level?

Start your day with a Star Memory for your Book of Stars. It'll change the whole day as well, and you then have the whole day and night to come on a different track from the get go.

It's a simple yet a wonderful change that is cumulative in its beneficial effects over time.

Sketching Star Memories

When we attempt to sketch a Star Memory, we engage a whole new system in our totality and often gain not only a new perspective on the memory, but also unlock further information in the process.

I invite you to try this for yourself; as long as you can manage a stick figure, you can do this too.

A tip: School art has a habit of traumatizing some children for life, if nothing is done about it. If you are absolutely reversed to even trying sketching a Star Memory, ask your dear Energy Mind to send you to a time and place, where an aspect absolutely loved playing with paints, or pencils, or even drawing something with their fingers in the sand – a re-connection to the native joy of creativity that is like a flame in young children, and then gets doused and doused again by the tedium and boredom of school art.

Stand up to this travesty and re-claim your flame of pure human creativity! You'll be so, so glad you did.

Raise energy, find the fun and joy in it, and just get started! This is my heartfelt wish for you!

Here's how to sketch a Star Memory.

1. Look through your Book of Stars and ask it to attract you to the perfect Star Memory that (needs?) to be further explored by making a sketch of it, a pictorial representation that is inherently different from a language based representation.

2. Use the Classic Game to step inside the memory and find the MOMENT.

3. Choose if you want to sketch the aspect having the moment from outside, or if you want to sketch what the aspect was seeing at the moment it happened.

4. What was the first important component in the scene?

- For example, an aspect was standing on the beach, looking at the moon over the water.

- The first important component is the moon. Feel across your paper where that needs to be placed so it feels exactly right. Use your 6th sense to find that place where X marks the spot.

- Draw the circle where it needs to be.

- Now ask, "What's the next component?" and the answer is, "The sea!"

- Again, feel for where the beach line and the horizon line need to be and draw two simple lines.

- Now we have the beach, and the moon – does this match the memory? Does it feel right? Make adjustments if necessary.

- "What else needs to be there?" In this example, the answer is, "The shimmering road of silver on the sea, leading to the moon!" We can represent that with two simple lines on the water.

- "And what else needs to be there?" The small shape of the aspect. Find where the right place is and draw a simple stick figure.

- "Anything else?" A few little bent lines to represent the dune grass as there was a sweet summer wind that was important to the experience.

- "Is this the right energy to represent the experience?" If the answer is yes, we're done! We have made a pictorial representation of a Star Memory.

- Now, spend some time to touch the drawing, and engage with the energy of the experience in this way. What have you noticed you never knew before? What can we learn/gain from having done this? Why was it important to sketch this one Star Memory out of all the possibilities – right here, right now? How can this help me, right here, right now?

Keep your sketches for future reference and as an ongoing source of support, information, inspiration as well as a clue to guide you into your own perfect future.

Star Matrix & SuperMind

SuperMind (the official public version of Project Sanctuary) transfers our consciousness from the Here & Now to the There & Then – into the energy worlds, in other words.

When we remember something, and consciously enter into it, this is an example of an energy world which we call "a habitat." Our dear Energy Mind creates this habitat for us, and we step inside and create whole new memories in doing so.

Our dear Energy Mind can create infinite worlds for us to experience lucidly, with all six senses, and we can have adventures and experiences, Star Events, in the energy worlds that we absolutely cannot have in physical reality.

As the energy body reacts to these experiences in the energy worlds exactly as it would to any experience we have anywhere, these Star Events are perfectly real and can be used for personal evolution.

For example, we can create Missing Events by taking an aspect to the perfect place in time and space where they can have the experiences we need to evolve, right here and now.

What's on many levels far more intriguing is to ask the dear Energy Mind to take us to the perfect place in time and space where we can experience a Star Event we need right now (as in, who we are presently, the current aspect).

We simply make the Set Up in the Heart Position and use the Classic Game to step inside that world or habitat, and follow the story along with, "And what happens next …?"

In every given group of people, 75% "don't get it" and dismiss this as "just fantasy, not for me," and that's alright.

I include SuperMind for the other 25% whose eyes light up and they can sense the enormous potential for fun, games and personal evolution that resides in our ability to live in two worlds, instead of just the one.

We are said to only use 5% of our brain power at this time. It is my assertion that the other 95% is there for computing the energy worlds, for travelling there, and for having true human experiences there that cannot be had in the Hard, no matter how hard or otherwise any one incarnation could possibly be.

I believe that learning to interact with our Star Memories will provide an entrance point to wanting to explore the true powers of our SuperMinds for many, many more, and that a time may come, where 100% of people's eyes light up when you say to them,

> *"Would you like to travel to the perfect place in time and space where you are going to experience a surprise Star Event that will evolve you ...?"*

This is my will! :-)

Star Matrix & The Energy Symbols

The 23 Energy Symbols were created to be a Rosetta Stone alphabet that both the Conscious Mind and the dear Energy Mind can understand.

The Energy Symbols can be used to access Star Memories about specific topics; to get an easy flow of Star Memories going; to practice Conscious Mind to Energy Mind communication; and to give the Energy Mind a chance to draw your attention to Star Memories that are particularly important or relevant to you, right here and now.

The Energy Symbols can also be used as a game with children, at a party, or at creativity sessions in a corporate environment. Their uses are literally infinite.

The Star Matrix Energy Symbols Pattern

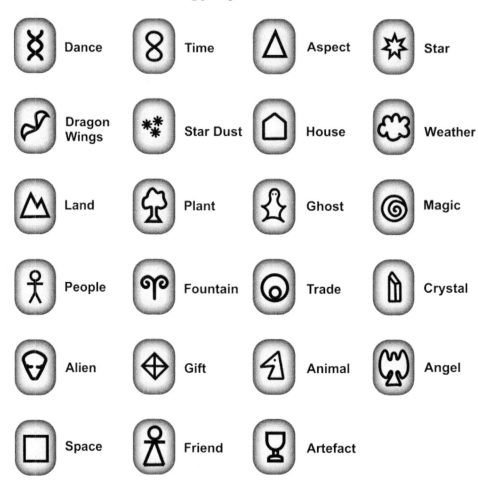

At the simplest level, we draw the symbols on material objects, such as pebbles or stones, and place them with the symbol side up in front of us.

We make the Set Up in the Heart Position as always.

- "Dear Energy Mind, please give me the perfect Star Memory for me today!" (or any Set Up of your choice).
- One of the symbols will attract our attention. We pick it up and look at it and the "memory download" will start.

- When it is complete, we say, "Thank you! Dear Energy Mind!" and return the symbol stone.

You can repeat this to get sequences of Star Memories that are connected/related and/or provide further information/help on your original Set Up.

This helps us connect Star Memories that we consciously did not understand that they needed to be connected, and gives our dear Energy Mind the opportunity to create a powerful sequence that leads to a real threshold shift.

We can use the Energy Symbols like a game to trigger Star Memories in others as well as in ourselves, because everyone's Energy Mind understands them. Children, old people, non-personal-development experienced people can all pick a stone and use it to "remind them of ..."

In a group, for example, we can take turns to tell "A funny story about ..." by picking a symbol. This is great fun and hugely energy raising.

Picking an Energy Symbol "at random" to get a Star Memory is something that we can do at any time and using the Energy Symbols in this way is particularly useful when you are feeling a bit down.

Each Energy Symbols is a theme "in its widest metaphorical sense." This gives our dear Energy Minds a really broad and wide remit to interpret the symbol, and use the symbol as a portal to send us the Star Memory that is just perfect for right here and now.

We can create sequences of Star Memories through using the symbols, and also cocktails, for example, we can choose 3 (or 5, or 7) Energy Symbols, each one will be a Star Memory, and they act together as "more than the sum of their parts."

As all the Energy Symbols are high Positives in their own right, they are particularly well suited to help us rediscover many, many more Star Memories across a huge range of contexts.

The Energy Symbols are a wonderful additional communications device to help us understand our own Energy Minds better, and I recommend them highly.

The Star Matrix Masters Course

Get up close and personal with your Star Memories, your Star Aspects, and gain a wonderful new sparkling self concept in this 12 Week, 12 Unit online Masters Course with Silvia Hartmann.

Created by your own life itself, Star Matrix is the most powerful personal development course in the world and the gift that will keep on giving.

The Star Matrix Masters course provides you with the structure and opportunity to discover core Star Memories in the right order and sequence, and to share tips, insights and energy with other Star Matrix explorers – Star People, as we like to call them. Sharing and receiving Star Memories is enormously empowering and infinitely educational in the truest and deepest sense.

Completing the Star Matrix Masters course will give you the mental, emotional and physical tools to enter a new phase of your life, far more in tune with your original mission, your destiny, and from a whole new vantage point of self awareness of the power you have held all along.

Upon course completion, you can joy the Star Matrix Forever group and dive deeper into the amazing applications of Star Matrix for healing, success creation, and for life.

It's time to discover the true Treasures & Riches of YOUR life – the time has come to start gathering in your harvest!

Details, dates, reviews and enrolment for The Star Matrix Masters Course with Silvia Hartmann is available here:

GoE.ac/StarMatrix

"I have discovered a whole new life I never knew I had!"

Star Matrix II Participant, at the end of course online meeting.

The Next Step

Join the Guild of Energists! Learn the core methods and techniques of Modern Energy and try out a treasure chest of practical methods and techniques to raise your energy with ...

The Modern Energy Foundation Online Video Course

Presented by Silvia Hartmann, Creator of Modern Energy and President, GoE.

- Unit 1: Why Your Happiness Matters!

The Introduction To Modern Energy

- Unit 2: EMO Energy In Motion

The Principles Of Modern Energy

- Unit 3: Modern Energy Tapping

Healing Events With The Power Of The Positives

- Unit 4: SuperMind

Infinite Creativity

- Unit 5: Modern Stress Management

The Trillion Dollar Stress Solution

- Unit 6: The Energy Of Relationships

Bonus Presentation with Alex Kent & Silvia Hartmann

Time limited access to this course comes free with this book! Gain YOUR Foundation Certificate in Modern Energy!

See page: 199

About The Guild Of Energists

In 1998, Silvia Hartmann created the first Modern Energy organisation to teach the 1st generation of modern energy based techniques which became The Guild of Energists as we know it today.

Modern Energy is The Third Field and Modern Energy professionals specialise in teaching people how to become happier by empowering the real, living human energy body with simple, logical and highly effective Modern Energy Techniques.

The Guild of Energists provides ongoing education, research and inspiration in Modern Energy and welcomes everyone who loves energy to join us in our mission to make people happier!

Modern Energy knowledge is of the essence to help people make sense of their lives, to heal from emotional/energetic wounds and disturbances, to unlock our true human abilities at the high energy states and to provides sound, logical Modern Energy theory as well as effective, beneficial, positive, humane and uplifting practice.

GoE members are transforming the lives of real people worldwide already every day!

Take part in a real Modern Energy event – they're awesome!

Find a GoE Energy Event: GoEe.ac/Events

Recommended Further Reading

Modern Energy Tapping – Silvia Hartmann

Start Unlocking The Power of the Positives in your life today!

DragonRising.com/store/METB/

EMO Energy In Motion – Silvia Hartmann

The theory and practice of the principles of Modern Energy

DragonRising.com/store/EMO/

The Energy of Attraction – Alex Kent

Applying the power of Modern Energy to Love, Dating and Relationships

DragonRising.com/store/the_energy_of_attraction/

Claim Your Star Matrix Certificate & Inclusive Bonuses

Thanks for purchasing Silvia Hartmann's Star Matrix – we wish you every success as you build up your own Book of Stars!

Every purchase of Silvia Hartmann's Star Matrix book comes complete with these fantastic bonuses[4]:

- Complete the Star Matrix online test and download your Star Matrix Foundation certificate

- 30 days GoE subscription including:

  - Star Matrix Summit online videos

  - GoE subscriber support forums and groups

  - GoE Modern Energy Foundation online video training course with Silvia Hartmann

---

4   The full list of bonuses is subject to change and we also regularly add more content to the GoE Digital Library for subscribers to enjoy! See GoE.ac/Library for an up-to-date list

- ○ GoE Energy Protection online video training course with Silvia Hartmann
- ○ Full access to the hundreds of videos, audio files and ebooks in the GoE Digital Library

How To Access Bonuses

If you've purchased the Star Matrix book direct from DragonRising Publishing or The GoE then you can simply login here using the details we emailed you:

- Complete Star Matrix Online Test – GoE.ac/SMXCert
- GoE Member Support Group – GoE.ac/Group
- Bonus videos and courses are in the GoE Digital Library - GoE.ac/Library

If you've purchased the Star Matrix book from another retailer such as Amazon, please confirm proof of purchase by writing a review of the book on their website, send us the link using our contact details below and we'll create an account for you to access the bonuses.

For more information, contact the GoE support team - GoE.ac/Contact

About The Author

Silvia Hartmann is the creator of Modern Energy and the President of The GoE, The Guild of Energists. Her original work includes:

1993 The Harmony Program
1996 Project Sanctuary
2000 Guiding Stars
2001 HypnoDreams
2002 EMO Energy In Motion
2003 Art Solutions
2004 Living Energy
2004 Energy Magic
2005 HypnoSolutions
2006 The Genius Symbols
2007 Aromatherapy For Your Soul

2008 Events Psychology
2009 Modern Energy Chart/SUE Scale
2009 The Genius Symbols
2012 Modern Energy Meditation
2013 Modern Stress Management
2014 Modern Energy Healing
2015 Modern Energy Tapping
2016 SuperMind
2018 (r)Evolution
2019 Star Matrix
2020 The Power of the Positives

"Love without logic is insanity. And vice versa."

SilviaHartmann.goe.ac

Printed in Great Britain
by Amazon

15818753R00119